™

TANKED™

THE OFFICIAL COMPANION

Wayde King and Brett Raymer

with David Bienenstock

LYONS PRESS
Guilford, Connecticut
An imprint of Globe Pequot Press

Lyons Press is an imprint of Globe Pequot Press.

See page 279 for photo credits and permissions.

Maps by Melissa Baker © Morris Book Publishing, LLC
Project editor: Meredith Dias
Text design: Sheryl P. Kober
Layout: Melissa Evarts

Library of Congress Cataloging-in-Publication Data is available on file.

ISBN 978-0-7627-9681-6

Printed in the United States of America

10 9 8 7 6 5 4 3 2 1

For everyone trying to preserve the marine environment one fish at a time, and for our amazing fans. We never could have imagined how well you would take to us and where the show has taken us.

CONTENTS

INTRODUCTION
The Family Business

When A-list celebrities like David Bowie, Kobe Bryant, Dr. Dre, Neil Patrick Harris, Tracy Morgan, Steven Spielberg, and Stephen Tyler decide to indulge a desire for a custom-built aquarium, they turn to the Acrylic Tank Manufacturing (ATM) factory and shop in Las Vegas, Nevada. That's because, working with the most cutting-edge machines and materials available anywhere on the planet, we're able to take our clients' completely over-the-top visions and translate them into stunning, underwater worlds of wonder, where fish, coral, and other marine life all flourish together in harmony.

> "All families, even those of modest means, should have access to the countless hours of entertainment and hands-on education that a well-constructed aquarium provides."

Housed within a 33,800-square-foot state-of-the-art facility, ATM has become the world's number-one provider of built-to-order aquariums. We design, manufacture, and assemble top-quality acrylic tanks of every size and shape, plus façades, filters, pumps, stands, and anything else you need. We do everything in-house, but we ship and install our tanks all over the world while working with responsible aquatic pet suppliers to fill them with healthy, happy fish and sea creatures.

With more than fifty employees working full time, ATM takes on over two hundred custom projects per year, ranging from 50 gallons to 1 million. The most compelling of these creations appear on *Tanked,* the hit show on Animal Planet, an incredible platform for our work that airs around the world, sharing one of the world's most popular and rewarding pastimes with millions of viewers.

As ATM's cofounders and the heads of this family business, we certainly enjoy all the attention, especially working with celebrity clients,

since high-profile aquarium aficionados often have thrillingly creative ideas. But we make sure to treat each and every one of our customers like a celebrity—not just those who happen to be famous actors, artists, athletes, or captains of industry. After all, we started out in this business not searching for fame and fortune but because we believe that all families, even those of modest means, should have access to the countless hours of entertainment and hands-on education that a well-constructed aquarium provides. The ATM team also loves to bring the beauty of the world's oceans, lakes, rivers, and streams into homes, offices, hospitals, public spaces, and even houses of worship. We think of what we make as living art, and we're thrilled to share it with the world.

Children especially can benefit from helping to take care of an aquarium, which provides an ongoing learning process that sparks their imaginations while providing a unique opportunity for parents to offer valuable, lasting lessons about responsibility, caretaking, and the delicate ecological balance required to create and maintain a healthy environment for aquatic creatures great and small. That's why we made sure to include a special section in this book that will help newcomers to this amazing hobby, with detailed instructions on how to plan and set up a simple starter tank at home, plus tips and tricks guaranteed to help out even the most experienced at-home enthusiasts.

Because when it comes to aquariums, there's always something new to discover: from the latest in pumps and filters to the ideal mix of fish, coral, and nutrients required to keep every critter in your tank happy and safe. We may be acknowledged experts in this field, but the entire ATM team understands that the day we stop learning is the day we begin to fall behind—and that's something we'll never let happen. Not when so many people from all over the world have come to rely on us not just as a source of information and inspiration but also as international ambassadors for the entire aquarium industry. With *Tanked* now airing literally all over the world, it's a responsibility we take very seriously, working long, hard hours to fulfill that role in the most conscientious manner possible.

Lest we lose track of the importance of our labors, every day our in-boxes fill up with hundreds of wonderful e-mails from satisfied customers and fans of the show. They explain in detail how aquariums have improved their lives and brought great happiness to their homes and families. Whether it's a personal note from the parents of an eight-year-old girl in Skokie, Illinois, who declared her intention to become a marine biologist after spending a few weeks setting up and maintaining a simple goldfish tank, or a quick thank you from a fifteen-year-old boy in Japan who loves watching the ATM staff play lighthearted pranks on one another, we read every message and in some way respond to them all as a way to say thank you to those who support us and the show. Nothing feels better than knowing we're bringing joy into the lives of literally millions of people.

> "Nothing feels better than knowing we're bringing joy into the lives of literally millions of people."

It's not just children who benefit from being near aquariums, though. According to a study conducted at Purdue University, elderly Alzheimer patients who interacted regularly with a fish tank for extended periods of time exhibited improved mental health and quality of life. Conducted by nursing professor Nancy Edwards, the study tracked sixty residents and found that those with steady exposure to an aquarium were more "relaxed and alert," ate up to 21 percent more food, and showed a marked decrease in wandering, yelling, pacing, and physical aggression. "I think the combination of movement, color, and sound provides a stimulating experience," Professor Edwards explained at the conclusion of the study. "Often long-term care environments do not offer a lot of stimulation, but fish move around in various patterns, so there's enough variability and visibility to keep patients' interest."

Additional research has proven that dental patients who spend time contemplating an aquarium prior to their session experience significantly less anxiety and discomfort than those shown just a poster of a similar underwater scene, which explains why so many of our custom-built tanks end up in the waiting areas of dentists, therapists, doctors, and other health professionals.

The orthodontist tank, featuring a great white shark getting his bite fixed

In the very first season of *Tanked,* we built a custom-designed aquarium meant to bolster the harmony of a couple's house by promoting the concept of feng shui, the art and science of arranging objects in accordance with the positive flow of energy, or qi, through space to promote wellness. Cultivating this kind of energy flow—a key principle of Chinese medicine for thousands of years—brings peace, health, and prosperity to all who enter such a well arranged environment. Feng shui also focuses on balancing a variety of objects, elements, and symbols that reflect the natural world, such as fire, wind, and (naturally) flowing water, which makes an aquarium a great fit for this style of design and helps explain why keeping fish has always been so popular throughout Asia.

It may have been old wisdom to some people, but the concept of feng shui was completely new to us when our clients first mentioned the idea.

But rather than shrink from the challenge or push them toward another, more familiar theme, we took it as an opportunity to learn something new that might improve the quality of our work while making the finished product more personal and meaningful for all involved. After hiring a local feng shui expert, we started our research with a crash course on how certain colors have distinct characteristics: Red, for example, possesses the kind of bright energy that brings good luck. Then we learned that where an aquarium resides, along with its relationship to other objects within that space, also greatly effects its feng shui. So we had to consider the size, shape, and positioning of the tank even more carefully than usual.

According to our expert advisor, water represents the containment of life force within the home, so ideally the tank should go at the center of the house, allowing that power to radiate throughout the structure, providing positive flow to all who dwell within. To keep that qi circulating properly, we built a complex filtration system called a refugium tank that drains dirty water from the main tank and moves it through mud, algae, and living sponges to clean it, replenishing it with healthy organisms along the way. This "bio-filtered" water then pumps back into the main tank, providing the fish with a consistent food supply.

We even matched the contents of the aquarium to the feng shui theme, starting with a living reef design in which everything in the tank works together to create a fully sustainable, self-regulating ecosystem. We filled the aquarium with flame scallops to represent red as the fire element, purple starfish to represent prosperity, and a mix of orange and white clownfish and anemones to illustrate the many symbiotic relationships found in nature, formed when diverse species interact in a mutually beneficial manner.

The Chinese symbol for water

When it came time to reveal the feng shui aquarium, with the *Tanked* cameras rolling, we all felt a little nervous about our attempt to integrate such age-old practices into our modern manufacturing and production methods. But in the end, the sense of flow and harmony we'd learned so much about clearly reflected in our work because the couple we built the aquarium for heartily

endorsed it. "I've had tanks before but nothing like this," James Lee told us with a beaming smile. "This reef tank is the total embodiment of balance between the rocks and the fish, and to have all of that within our own home is just amazing!"

"Now, when you're in this room, the energy just flows all around you," his wife, Joyce, added. "It's a very positive energy."

> "If you can dream it, we can build it."

Creating that kind of positive energy is the mission we bring to every custom-build job. Whether it's a small and sedate in-home aquarium for a couple like the Lees or a massive, awe-inspiring 70,000-gallon New Testament–themed tank for the IBOC megachurch in Dallas—it's all about producing a harmonious flow among ourselves, the clients, and the fish. We strive not just to satisfy our customers' expectations but to exceed them, going beyond what they can envision or anticipate until we create a work of living art at which they will gaze in wide-eyed wonder for the rest of their lives.

Obviously, we don't typically need to hire an outside expert and consult the wisdom of the ancients to achieve that goal, but we're always willing to go the extra mile and do whatever it takes to make our tanks truly unforgettable. We believe there's no such thing as a "perfect" aquarium, but, given enough time and an adequate budget, we can definitely build the perfect aquarium for you. That's why, at the beginning of each episode of *Tanked,* we make one simple promise: If you can dream it, we can build it. Fulfilling that promise and seeing the joy that our aquariums bring into the world make all the hard work of running the world's number-one aquarium manufacturing company and starring in our own television show worth the time and effort. So don't worry: No matter where this amazing journey takes us next, we'll always think of ourselves as just two fish guys from New York lucky enough to spend every day doing what we love. Our clients and the fans who watch *Tanked* are what make all of that possible, so, on behalf of our families and everyone at ATM:

Tanks so much!

Wayde Brett

MEET THE ATM TEAM

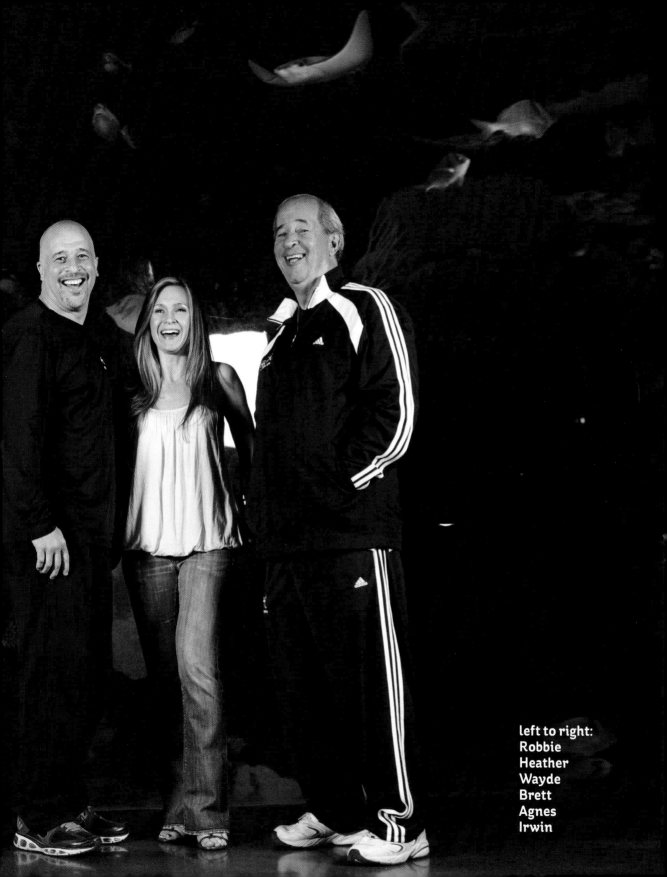

left to right:
Robbie
Heather
Wayde
Brett
Agnes
Irwin

WAYDE

I was born on Long Island, New York, in 1966 and have spent pretty much my entire life taking care of aquariums, a passion—later a career—I first learned from my mother and stepfather. In a household including five sisters and me, our family never had much money, but at any given moment we had every type of animal imaginable living under our roof, including fish, birds, snakes, lizards, and one iguana so exotic that it didn't have a proper name yet in the United States.

My mother raised guppies when she was twelve years old, and my uncle later worked for the government, setting up US post offices around the world to handle international mail, and every time he traveled somewhere far flung he brought back strange fish and other creatures that ended up in our basement. My parents sold them to local pet stores to help pay the bills. During my youngest years, I thought of all those wondrous animals as my pets. Later I learned they were really our guests—all part of our family business.

Today I oversee my own family business, working with my brother-in-law Brett; my father-in-law, Irwin; and my wife, Heather, to run ATM. The global reach of our television show, *Tanked,* has helped us, after nearly two decades in business, to grow into the world's number-one custom aquarium provider, but we still have the strong roots and tight bonds of family at our core.

Back when I was a kid, though, my parents' business was a much more traditional mom-and-pop operation, struggling just to get by and make ends meet. My stepfather, Shelly, started the first commercial aquarium service company in New York in 1964 and toiled tirelessly to make it a success. He had a great heart and treated my mother like a queen, so I always respected him and wanted to earn his respect in return. I started at home by helping to raise piranhas, red devils, wolf pikes, and even some freshwater fish that are now illegal.

Living every day among the tanks that filled our basement and even my bedroom taught me that fish require just as much attention as any other pet. I developed the sense of responsibility that came with taking care of them. A whole new world called to me from inside those tanks, and I needed to know everything about it. I read everything on the subject until I knew how to set up the tanks and the filtration systems myself. When my fish got sick, I studied them carefully to determine what went wrong and how to fix it. As a result, I became almost neurotic about cleanliness, creating my own schedule to wipe down all the tanks under my supervision. From very early on, I was always extremely hands-on with my aquariums, trying different, creative ways of setting them up and caring for them.

When I became a teenager, to keep me out of trouble and off the streets, my stepfather started taking me with him when he went out to service aquariums. I started at the bottom, wiping down tanks until they were perfectly clean and transparent. Shelly taught me a lot as we labored side-by-side—not just about aquariums and the pet supply industry but about life and how to conduct myself in an honorable way at all times. He introduced me to every facet of his operation, making sure I mastered each step before moving on to the next. Before long I understood not just how to take care of fish and tanks but also bookkeeping, sales, and customer service, skills I use every day today.

I always learn best when a lesson is hands-on, so, looking back, that was the perfect kind of education to keep me interested. Also, seeing the pride Shelly took in the smallest details of his work made a major impression on me. In fact, to this day, no matter how many custom aquariums we have in production, and despite the rigorous demands of running ATM and

Me in my younger days when I was first learning the aquarium business

filming *Tanked* simultaneously, I still personally approve every job before it ships out to ensure it meets the high standards I demand of myself and my colleagues. I notice everything, and if I don't like what I see I'm going to have it redone. I don't care what it costs.

Years ago, when we first implemented this protocol, I had to send things back with some frequency, but now my guys know not to come to me with anything less than perfection. When we started, ATM was a small shop, and I did a lot of the work myself, but now that's no longer possible. A big part of my job today consists of figuring out my employees' strengths and weaknesses and engaging them accordingly. One might be the worst acrylic polisher in the world but a great organizer and motivator. Some folks work hard out on the road, and others fall apart. I've moved employees from plumbing to coral inserts and found that they're ten times better in the new position. You have to be open minded and take chances on people, see how they do.

Through trial and error we've built an incredible team of skilled artisans who are the best in their respective fields, so I now have four or five guys

whom I can let loose on a job site without worrying about any major catastrophes. Although, as you can see in almost every episode of *Tanked,* nothing ever runs as smoothly as you'd like—no matter how long you've been at it.

Our knowledge and experience really pays off, though, when dealing with the inevitable routine setbacks. For example, when Brett and I were installing Neil Patrick Harris's Harry Houdini tank at the world-famous Magic Castle in Los Angeles (see page 162), a valve leak developed. No big deal if it's just a couple of guys doing routine plumbing—a twenty-minute fix, maybe—but when you're standing next to one of the world's most celebrated actors with two

Nervously unveiling the Magic Castle tank for Neil Patrick Harris (see page 162)

cameras capturing every move you make for a million people, it suddenly becomes all too easy to panic. If we hadn't been through that sort of thing so many times before, who knows what could have happened?

Meanwhile, I can also look back on my younger days and see how the many advantages of working with family inspired me ultimately to do the same as an adult, which ended up being one of the best decisions of my life. It's hard to keep certain employees in line when they know you can't fire them, and we all have a hard time separating our work lives and home lives, but those feel like small disadvantages when compared to having people around me I can trust absolutely, who

> "My guys know not to come to me with anything less than perfection."

understand me so well and care about me so deeply. Not that things always go smoothly when dealing with family—or ever go smoothly, I guess.

If you watch the show regularly, you know that Brett and I often disagree on matters both personal and professional, and sometimes we get into screaming matches that non–New Yorkers often misconstrue as vicious fighting. But underneath the noise, trust and mutual respect keep

us working together and bring out the best in each of us. You don't always see it on television, but ten minutes after one of our five-alarm blowups we're invariably back to joking around without a second thought (or an apology)—a transition possible only because we're much more than just business partners.

Meanwhile, my father-in-law, Irwin, aka the General, has served as a mentor to me in the business world and as an integral part of ATM's brain trust. He also has my back no matter what. He treats me like a son, so I try to take care of him like a father. The most important way I can do that is by being the best husband possible for his daughter, my wife, Heather, who, in her own way, has also contributed mightily to ATM's success.

Even Agnes, our estimator, and Robbie "the Redneck," our resident marine technician, feel like part of the family after so many years of working together, sharing the highs and lows of this wild ride. I really do think of the entire ATM team as one big extended family . . . but fortunately I don't have to go home and live with all fifty of them at the end of the day! Just my wife and my father-in-law, with whom I share a large house on the outskirts of Las Vegas. In fact, as you'll see, the construction of that house played a key role in bringing us all together to make this family business in the first place.

So, yes, despite having a bigger company to operate than my parents ever could have dreamed, I still get that same warm feeling of love and respect every time I step into the office. Like many working people, I spend a lot more of my waking hours there than at home. With so many responsibilities, so many plates to keep spinning at once, and an insatiable drive to make sure ATM remains at the pinnacle of the aquarium industry, I typically work ten to twelve hours per day, sometimes seven days a week. Which means having my family around me at the office is actually the best way to make sure we spend quality time together.

That might not work for every family, but it works for us, and it worked for my parents back in their day. Warmest among my childhood memories are the nights when we'd load up the car with all our tank equipment and head to a large restaurant on the south shore of Long Island. It housed maybe forty beautiful aquariums, lining every wall, filled with triggers,

Stuck behind my desk, but at least I'm dressed comfortably!

lionfish, and many other saltwater varieties. At midnight, after the restaurant closed, we went in and cleaned them.

So there I was, just a young kid, wide awake in the middle of the night, trying to help my parents make a living. This restaurant owner was very particular and wanted his aquariums to look perfect, so we went through with all our buckets and hoses, draining each and every tank one by one. Then we vacuumed the gravel and wiped the glass down thoroughly. We had it down to a routine, but it was still hard physical work that took hours to complete. When we started, I thought of it as just a job, but the older I got the more I considered it as a career.

But first, like most young people, I wanted to strike out on my own. I headed down to South Florida and started a valet business. Then I trained

to become a tool machinist, learning skills that served me well when it came time to learn how to shape acrylic into custom aquariums. From there, I progressed to the American Institute of Diamond Cutting. With that

Me in a tie . . . a rare sight!

sought-after skill under my belt, I entered the jewelry business. I worked with a man named Mark Cohen, a great influence on me in every way. He taught me the ins and outs of business and became a father figure to me. Cutting stones at a bustling shop in my old neighborhood back in Long Island made me good money, I loved my boss, and there was room to advance, but in the back of my mind I always wanted to return to my first love: the pet fish industry.

OK, I'll admit it: Having to wear a suit and tie every day bothered me. I mean, I'm a hands-on guy, so I never really saw myself sitting behind a desk in uncomfortable clothes. Luckily, these days, as the boss of my own rapidly expanding empire, I may be stuck behind my desk more than I'd like, dealing with phone calls, e-mails, and invoices, but at least I can do that while wearing shorts and a T-shirt. Everyone who works here feels free to do the same, and the casual dress code proves particularly popular in the summer when temperatures in Las Vegas routinely climb above 100 degrees.

My other so-called "fashion" statement involves the hundreds of pairs of sneakers that I've accumulated over the past few years. I used to like immaculate white sneakers—I'm a meticulous, clean-freak kind of guy, so no surprise there—but lately I'm getting into some wilder fluorescent colors. I'm not a collector, though; I don't seek out the rarest designer limited-edition pairs and put them on a shelf. I wear pretty much every pair that I buy. It all goes back to high school. Kids made fun of my ripped sneakers. Eventually it got so bad that my toes stuck through, but I still had to wear them, even in the winter, because I couldn't afford a new pair, slipping around in old, beat up, worn out kicks. It sounds kind of silly now, but it was a big deal to me at the time. As soon as I could afford new sneakers, I bought a new pair . . . and never stopped. Each new pair is a little gift to myself.

The Dwyane Wade pop-up sneaker stingray tank

Now, don't get me wrong: I like to enjoy life, but I'm not into extravagance for its own sake or trying to live some kind of celebrity lifestyle. It's just not who I am or what I want out of my time on Earth. Like most guys, I do love fancy motorcycles and fast cars, though. I have my father's old '65 Super Sport Malibu, all original, and in such great condition that it's been in a few hundred movies set back then. (It's on a registered list that filmmakers consult when they need old cars for their backgrounds.) I also have a Porsche Carrera 996 with a twin turbo engine. My everyday car is a black Chrysler 300 SRT8, which I love.

The Carrera 996 that brought Agnes into the ATM family

All of these perks came along only recently, though, when finally I was able to enjoy the fruits of my labor. The truth is: It's been a long, difficult journey in the aquarium business with a lot of major ups and downs along the way. In 2008, during the worst of the Great Recession, we had to lay off dozens of employees, many of them close friends, and we almost lost ATM entirely amid the larger credit crunch. Trusted employees embezzled from us, and we lost millions of dollars because certain clients for whom we busted our butts decided not to pay their bills.

My Chrysler 300

Still, to sit here now, watching my dreams come true and looking forward to an even brighter future, I have to look back on my decision to leave the jewelry business as fate. The only problem, once I made up my mind to make the move, was how to get my feet wet. I'd succeeded in a variety of different fields since leaving home, but my only reference in the aquarium world happened to be my own mother. She contacted one of her long-term suppliers, a tank manufacturer out in San Diego, and they offered me a position based solely on her word. (Thanks, Mom!) An exciting new job in my chosen field, plus all the sun, sand, and surf of one of Southern California's premier beach towns . . . what more could a young man want?

> "We almost lost ATM entirely amid the larger credit crunch."

Just one problem: Less than a month after I moved from one coast to the other, my new employer announced his plan to pull up stakes and move the entire operation to Las Vegas. It was a major bummer, as the San Diego surfers would have phrased it, but nothing was keeping me in California, so I decided to follow my new job into the desert . . . and I'm glad I did. Not because it was a great opportunity to get ahead—the company went bankrupt and closed within a year—but because that's where I found my wonderful wife, Heather, who's made my life complete and inspired my every move since the moment I laid eyes on her.

But first I met her father, the General. Talk about Beauty and the Beast!

Seriously, though, I initially came into contact with the Raymer family when Irwin contacted the company where I worked to order a custom aquarium for the new dream home that he and his wife started building in 1994 to live out their golden years. The General grew up poor in New York like me—much poorer in fact—then made his fortune as a salesman, so he wanted his new place to have everything he'd ever wanted and to be able to share it with his family. It's a dream anybody can relate to, but he was fortunate enough to be living it.

The company went belly up before we could finish his custom aquarium, so I ended up cutting a side deal to make it myself as a private contractor with the provision that he let me work in the garage of his

still-under-construction dream house. Naturally I offered him a good deal for the inconvenience, and there's nothing the General loves better than a bargain, so we shook hands, and I got to work right away building a beautiful 600-gallon wall tank between his living room and dining room that's still there today. It was a big job for just one guy, which meant becoming a regular presence in the General's home for a few weeks. I didn't know it at the time, but that arrangement changed the rest of my life.

> "There's nothing the General loves better than a bargain."

It all started, during one of my earliest visits to the house, when I noticed a picture of my future bride in the living room. I'd already made a good impression on Heather's mother, so I asked her a few innocent questions, hoping she'd put in a good word on my behalf. Heather was seeing someone else at the time, though, so I ended up on a date with her sister. A lovely woman, but I was determined that Heather would be mine—a feeling that only grew once we finally met and then slowly got to know each other during my frequent visits to work on her dad's aquarium.

Before long, I started making up reasons to stop by when I thought she might be home. We started as friends, but, when she broke up with her boyfriend, I told her we were meant to be together. Eventually we crossed the line from friendship to love, and we've never looked back. Heather can tell that story much better than I can, and I'm sure she will, so I'll just say that what I like best about her is that she always knows exactly what she wants in life and isn't shy about telling me how to help her make it happen.

Nor does she take crap from anybody, myself included, which I really respect. The old saying goes that behind every great man there's a great woman, but I don't believe that for a minute. I say that *beside* every great man there's a great woman. Heather is and always will be my equal partner in our marriage, even if I'm in charge at work and she's in charge at home. She's also the most amazing mother to our two wonderful daughters, Taylor and Morgan. Working so many long hours, I love knowing that she's always there for the girls, no matter what.

Heather also put in her time at ATM. She used to work a lot more, back when we first got married. In those days, with no kids and a fledgling new business, we needed all hands on deck just to make sure we survived the first year. ATM opened for business a few months before our wedding. It all started when Irwin saw the excellent job I did on his aquarium and learned how much experience I had in the industry, going back to my childhood. We talked about buying the bankrupt company where I used to work and turning it into something new, something groundbreaking. Even in the short time I was there, I knew the business could be profitable with some long-overdue changes, but I lacked the capital to buy it and bring that vision to life.

He was about to retire, but the General smelled a good investment opportunity. A lifelong entrepreneur, he couldn't ignore it. No doubt he also liked the idea of setting up his daughter and her fiancé in a business that hopefully would take care of us and our children long after he was gone. Irwin loves a deal, but he also understands that money is worth only what you spend it on. In this case, that meant making a large investment in his own family.

Which is where Brett enters the picture. We're now both friends and family, but back then he really didn't like me—and the feeling was somewhat mutual. As Heather's older brother, he had always been protective of her, going back to their Brooklyn days, and now here was some guy he hardly knew coming in to take over that role. We're both highly competitive, but with diametrically opposed out-looks on life, so the two of us getting off on the wrong foot seemed almost inevitable. Imagine my surprise, then, when the General offered to put up the money to start ATM on the condition that Brett serve as president of the company!

Not long after, I formally assumed that title—since I had been doing it from the very beginning—but in all honesty, even though I still bust his chops on TV, Brett works extremely hard now at making our business and *Tanked* an ongoing success. But back then he was still kind of an irresponsible kid, used to getting by on charm. Don't get me wrong, Brett's

My future brother-in-law and me on my big day

an extremely bright guy, and even in those days, whenever he put his mind to something, he did great. It just didn't happen all that often. Which led to a lot of bitter feuds between us during the lean early years of our "arranged marriage" in the aquarium industry.

ATM started with just six employees, including Brett, Heather, and me. We had such a small staff that it was hard to stay on top of everything. I was doing all the hands-on work during the day and then trying to catch up on paperwork at night. It was grueling. Naturally I resented when Brett waltzed into the office a few hours late after spending the night partying on the Las Vegas strip.

But after a few years, he finally realized that nothing's more important than a family that loves and supports you, which in our case included the family business. It was an epiphany for him. I mean, he's still the same fun-loving, enthusiastic, wisecracking guy that people love to be around, but now he makes that work for him by channeling that amazing energy into his job. He's also the main reason that the idea for the TV show got off the ground in the first place—which I'm sure he'll say more than makes up for his past shortcomings!

Long before the first episode of *Tanked* ever aired, ATM stood apart because of the amazing strength, clarity, and versatility of the acrylic tanks we build. We also established an Internet presence early, thanks to a friend and later employee who happened to learn web design a few years before the rest of the world. Even with those key innovations, however, our success was hard fought and hard won. It took a long time to climb out of the sizable debt we took on just to open our doors. We also had a pretty steep learning curve that led to some expensive missteps. Still, we got a lot more right than we got wrong, and in time ATM grew to more than fifty employees

and moved to a larger manufacturing space and then an even larger one. We take great pride in creating high-paying manufacturing jobs in our own community while making a name for ourselves around the world.

Then, in 2008, the misdeeds of a bunch of Wall Street bankers threatened to wash away everything we'd struggled to build for more than a decade. I mean, let's face it: As much as I love aquariums, they're not exactly up there with food and shelter when it comes to the necessities of survival. When the first terrible wave of financial panic hit in September of that year, we lost a huge number of standing orders overnight as people and businesses cut overhead as quickly as possible. Then the dysfunctional credit markets made it next to impossible to collect on outstanding bills.

To put it plainly: People owed us millions, and we owed millions to other people. It was a dire situation. Brett started working really hard. Heather returned to the office after leaving to be a full-time mother. Even Irwin came out of retirement to help us weather the storm and right our ship, starting with a new investment in ATM to get us through our short-term liquidity problem. But he did so much more than that. He helped us sharpen our pencils so we could stay on top of payroll, inventory, collections, accounting, bookkeeping—everything.

Meanwhile, building projects all over the world stopped. Nobody was ordering new tanks. We fought among ourselves and struggled to stay open. But everybody saw the light at the end of the tunnel. We all knew it was a viable business that ultimately would be successful if we could just ride out the rough patch.

Then, slowly, the economy started to recover, and the Internet helped us land some international jobs to make up for the gap in domestic orders. The aquarium market overall still hasn't bounced back to where it was ten years ago, however. Fewer people are buying, and those who do increasingly demand a bargain. So we find ourselves working a lot harder to make the same dollar.

Still, I gotta admit—and Brett's gonna love reading this—once *Tanked* took off, our sales shot up almost exponentially. We've been working at or near full capacity ever since the show began airing, with at least two to three custom tanks in production at any given time and more than ten thousand

At first, I worried about our arguments being broadcast around the world.

already sold and successfully installed. To keep up with demand, we just moved into a brand new, state-of-the-art facility with a 33,800-square-foot manufacturing plant, of which 9,000 square feet are office space—all under one roof. We also have a retail facility open to the public, including the hundreds of *Tanked* fans who come by every week to take the tour, meet the staff, and watch us make aquariums.

Many of them are surprised to find that I'm really here, in the ATM office, on the day they happen to show up. Which invariably makes me laugh because I'm always here—unless I'm on the road overseeing a complicated installation. Lest you think that my life's all glitz and glamour now that we're on TV, I spent my last birthday in the freezing cold and pouring rain in upstate New York plumbing a basement aquarium.

Despite the show's success, our family hasn't changed much. We still work the same jobs and have the same problems—just now a lot more people know about them. During the first season of *Tanked*, I worried a lot about our arguments being broadcast around the world, but now that I've had a chance to meet and talk with so many fans over the last few years, I'm convinced that, if anything, seeing us that way, warts and all, only makes us more relatable.

We're normal people who make extraordinary aquariums, and you guys get that. Which explains why the most common question I'm asked isn't "How can you put up with Brett's awful jokes?" (Gotcha, buddy!), but which ATM aquarium is my favorite. That's kind of like asking me to pick my favorite child, so I usually switch things around and ask fans to tell me their favorites instead. It's a great conversation starter, and it helps me better understand what you find appealing about our tanks so we can show more of what you want in the future.

> "We're normal people who make extraordinary aquariums."

I also love that the tour groups and our social media pages allow me to interact with so many young people who explain how the show has inspired them to learn about aquariums, marine life, and how to protect our fragile oceans. I try to encourage them in every way possible because, who knows, maybe one of those kids will come up with some innovation that saves the world!

In the meantime, I'll never forget when I realized that *Tanked* was becoming a cultural phenomenon and that our lives would never be the same. I mean, we literally got eight thousand e-mails the day after the first episode aired, which was staggering at the time, and people started to recognize Brett and me in public pretty much right away, but that sort of thing is really no big deal once you get used to it, especially in small doses.

No, the moment came in the middle of the second season. The public was just starting to get behind the show in a big way, and momentum was building on its own. Then, one afternoon, the owners of the Detroit Tigers invited us to game and provided us amazing seats. You have to understand: Brett's a total sports fanatic.

> "We literally got eight thousand e-mails the day after the first episode aired."

If he put his mind to business as he does to sports, we'd have been millionaires long ago. But I can barely tell the difference between a home run and a double-play. You probably think I'm exaggerating, but it's true.

Before the game even started, some guys came out onto the field with a metal fence that they were pulling behind a tractor, and I asked Brett what was going on. He explained that they were grooming the infield so the ball would bounce smoothly, and the people around us couldn't believe how little I knew for someone sitting in the third row—but then again I probably know more about aquariums than anyone in the world!

I didn't let that bother me, though. It was a brand new, beautifully built stadium, and I got into the excitement of my first ever baseball game. For once in my life, I wasn't thinking about work at all. Until someone called my name, and then Brett's name. I looked back, and a guy was pointing at us. The crowd began to buzz, and soon people started pouring down from the stands, wanting to take pictures. Eventually, stadium security and the police came and asked us to disperse the crowd. But we were just sitting there. What could we do?

The first baseman looked at me and just shrugged his shoulders. In a way, it was kind of embarrassing. He's the famous baseball player, but here we were getting all of this attention. That's when it hit home for me. The game got even wilder an inning later when Brett caught a foul ball. He just reached up and snagged it. Apparently the guy sitting behind him had been waiting for that chance for ten years, had his glove ready and everything. He was probably pretty upset, but you know Brett, that didn't stop him from holding up his souvenir for the whole stadium to see.

> "In the end, security had to escort us out. When we finally made it back to the car, I got hot and cold chills."

After the game, fans lined up outside our section hoping to say hello. In the end, security had to escort us out. When we finally made it back to the car, I got hot and cold chills. So many people wanting to shake our hands or just say something nice about the show had been a truly surreal experience.

Of course, the flip side to all that positive attention is having to deal with our fair share of detractors, sometimes in person, but mostly online. Typically they mean well but don't understand that you can't build an aquarium, ship it cross-country, install it, and fill it with fish in forty-four minutes. Sometimes they make assumptions, and even accusations, without knowing how much we do to make sure the animals we work with get treated properly at all times. They don't know all the precautions we take behind the scenes or that we've actually shut down filming several different times until the fish acclimated fully to their new environments. That kind of footage doesn't always end up on TV.

Nor do most people realize how much production goes into an episode of *Tanked.* The TV crew shoots up to eighty hours of footage to make just one episode. There's absolutely no script, and we never know what will make it into the show until the night it airs. We all get together to watch it as a family, just like everyone else. At first that made me nervous, but now I find it exciting, especially seeing what took place when I wasn't around.

> "The TV crew shoots up to eighty hours of footage to make just one episode."

The show has definitely improved with each new season, which is also really satisfying. Along the way, I've tried to teach the production team everything possible about our business while learning as much as I can from them about how to shoot a TV show. The more we all know, the better we can pull together to get the footage they need without disrupting everyone's lives. It's nice to be on a hit TV show so I can show the world the wonderful custom aquariums that we build; we don't build them just to get on television. In the meantime, with ATM, *Tanked,* and my family, three very demanding worlds all overlap. Most people couldn't sit in my seat and not go crazy, but I wouldn't trade it for the world—not the success, not the struggle.

People may look at me now and see a TV star with a thriving business and nice cars, but they don't realize what I've gone through to get here. I still don't have a life of leisure like some of my friends who have very little

The illustrious founder

money. I've got too many responsibilities, too many people depending on me—starting with my wife and two children—to take a day off, never mind a vacation. Some people build a business, and when they die it's gone, but I don't want that to happen to ATM. I want the people who work here decades down the line to look up at a portrait of me on the wall and remember me as the illustrious founder who busted his ass building the company and keeping it vital.

If my daughters decide to learn the aquarium business and take over ATM, I would love that. I'd teach them everything I know and help them get started. I could even keep an office for myself and act as an advisor, the same way the General offers us all the benefit of his logic and experience today. If that's what *they* want, that would be great, but, if my girls would rather be doctors, lawyers, or marine biologists, then that's what they should do. They have their own minds and need to follow their own paths in life, pursuing their own happiness—whether in their jobs, relationships, friendships, sports, whatever they choose. They're going to have good times and bad, great successes and disappointments, and they're going to get their hearts broken. I grew up with five sisters, so I know what to expect.

As for me, I'm not sure I'm the type of guy who can ever really retire. Even when I was younger, I always imagined myself working in my old age, like sitting in a booth as a security guard. Maybe I could be the night watchman at ATM . . .

Guess you'll just have to keep tuning in to *Tanked* to find out!

Wayde King
Founder, President, and CEO of ATM

BRETT

I grew up in Brooklyn, and, even if I live

out the rest of my days in Las Vegas,

I'll never let go of my New York attitude.

That's one of the things about *Tanked* that people really

respond to—a bunch of fish-out-of-water New Yorkers

building amazing aquariums in the middle of the desert.

We're completely displaced, yet we fit right in, and we're

not afraid to get in your face should the need arise.

• • •

The Big Apple faced some tough times when I was a kid, but my father did well after starting up his own business, so we always had everything we needed and a little more. You probably know him best as "the General," but Dad's actually a gentle soul, especially when it comes to his family. He's always been there for me, whenever I needed him, and I love him to death for that. Our relationship has definitely had its ups and downs over the years, but now that the show's a hit, our business is thriving, and I'm pulling my weight around the office, we're actually closer than ever before.

Growing up, we had an aquarium in the house with a bunch of oscars in it, but to be honest I never paid it much mind. I liked to watch the fish swim around, but that's where my interest ended. Cleaning tanks wasn't really my thing, so I left that for my siblings.

My first love was sports. A natural athlete, I excelled at baseball, football, swimming, and tennis. As you've seen on the show, I've always had a competitive spirit when properly motivated, and nothing brought that out like the thrill of hearing a crowd cheering from the sidelines—even if it was just a couple dozen parents watching a Little League game. I've been telling

people all my life that I'd be famous someday for something, but most of them didn't think it would ever happen.

I could always count on my sister, Heather, to believe in me, though. I'm six years older than she is, and I know that she used to look up to me a lot when we were kids. We've been close for as long as I can remember. I still feel protective of her, even to this day. After all, I've done everything from changing her diaper and wheeling her around in a stroller to teaching her how to do the backstroke and now working alongside her. In return, she has always made me feel like a celebrity, even when nobody else did. Knowing that so much affection and admiration are coming at me from one of my favorite people in the world makes it all the more special.

My first chance at actual fame came when I was still quite young. A couple of scouts from a prestigious swim academy in Florida saw me compete and approached my parents about enrolling me into an intensive training program that could have put me on a path to the Olympics. But it would have meant leaving school for private tutors and spending most of the year away from home, so ultimately we declined their offer. It was a difficult decision at the time, though one I don't regret. I preferred football and

Swim champ!

basketball anyway, so that's where all of my energies went . . . until in my senior year at Lincoln High I tore the anterior cruciate ligament in my knee and came crashing back down to Earth.

I graduated and from there I went to the State University of New York in Stony Brook to study liberal arts. My father decided to retire early, leave Brooklyn, and build a home in Las Vegas, and before long our whole family was living out there with him, except for me. I stuck around the old neighborhood even after college, earning decent money as a bartender while trying to start my own business. Those were fun days, when I was young and carefree, and I made the most of them. But I missed my family and worried that I wasn't living up to my potential. I mean, there aren't that many famous bartenders.

Playing football at Lincoln High—go Railsplitters!

Then, in the winter of 1994, when I was twenty-four years old, a ferocious blizzard hit New York City, closing the airports, freezing the sidewalks, and pushing snow two feet high into the crosswalks. The next morning, I went out to stock up on some provisions, and the bitter wind whipping through the streets brought stinging tears to my eyes. Then I stepped ankle-deep into a puddle of melted ice that left my foot soaking wet in the freezing cold. Relocating to Las Vegas started to sound like a marvelous idea.

I've always enjoyed visiting new places and having adventures, so why not? Brooklyn wasn't going anywhere, and if I didn't have good luck in Sin City I could always do a 180 and head right back home. As it turned out, however, I probably ended up liking my new surroundings a little too

much when I first arrived. You could even say that I fell into what locals call the "Vegas trap" of trying to keep up with the high rollers.

Since I had experience as a bartender and knew a lot about sports, I made plans to open my own sports bar. I started scouting locations right away and talked to my dad about being my business partner. But this was right around the time that Heather and Wayde got together, and my plans didn't develop as I'd hoped. I guess it's true what John Lennon said: "Life is what happens when you're busy making other plans."

To be honest, I didn't like Wayde at first. Well, the first time I met him it was just a quick-introduction-and-hello kind of thing. He was just some guy my father hired to build an aquarium in our house. But then he was hanging around more and more, and I eventually caught wind that he had designs on my little sister. Heather was only nineteen at the time, and she'd just gotten out of a long relationship with her high school sweetheart, so I didn't appreciate a thirty-year-old man making a play for her. Nearly twenty years later, they're still so happy together, and I see what a great husband and father Wayde is, but at the time I didn't know him at all, so I didn't trust him. Also, as I said, I've always been protective of Heather, even now that we're both adults with kids of our own. Some things never change and probably shouldn't.

> "To be honest, I didn't like Wayde at first."

When my father decided to put up the money to start ATM, he made me the president of the company so I could keep a close eye on his investment. Wayde and I went from adversaries to business partners overnight. Dad likes to say that his logic outdoes most people's knowledge, and that decision really proves his point. At first, Wayde and I had a rough time learning to rely on each other, with a lot of disagreements along the way, but ultimately we worked it out. So now, instead of potentially having a rift between his children and factions within the business, we're all one big happy family. Pretty clever, General!

We had such a small staff when we first started and so much to do that we all wore a lot of hats, often working on every step of a given tank, from conception and manufacturing to installation and filling it with fish, at the

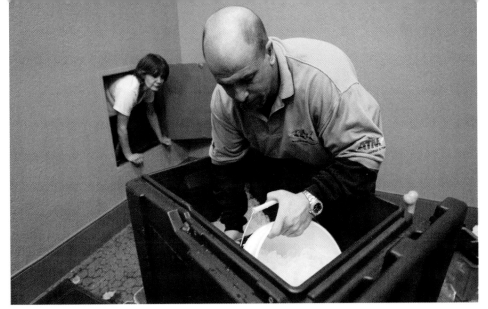

Hard at work on the Mob Experience tank installation (see page 116)

same time—or as I like to say: everything from selling to sanding. In a way, each episode of *Tanked* takes me back to those days because to fulfill the premise of the show we bring viewers through all those same steps.

These days, as America's leading custom aquarium supplier, with more than fifty employees, we build way too many tanks for Wayde and me to show up personally at every install site, so, working with the producers of the show, we select certain builds that we hope will appeal to you guys, and we focus on documenting them from start to finish. A lot of people actually ask me how we pick which tanks to film—particularly potential clients hoping to make it onto the show—so here's what we're looking for when it comes to getting on the air.

First and foremost, you've got to have a compelling story, something unique that we've never done before. Like the small oyster shell aquarium that was part of a marriage proposal or the tank we built at a local Las Vegas tattoo

> "You've got to have a compelling story."

parlor to soothe nervous customers before they get inked. We're also looking for clients with a budget large enough to make something with a cool, creative concept or off-the-wall theme, which usually starts around $20,000. You also have to have a great personality that will come across

on television. If you think you can put all that together, give us a call at the office, and let's talk!

My other most frequently asked question is: How did *Tanked* get on television in the first place? Luckily that's a story that I love to tell.

ATM started up just a few months before Wayde and Heather got married in 1998, and at the time just half a dozen of us worked for the company. We had a bullpen set-up in the office, our desks pushed together so we could all yell out to one another whenever we had a question or needed to pass along info. At any given moment, we all were talking, laughing, teasing, pranking, fighting, and having every manner of crazy interaction imaginable. Clients, suppliers, and friends encountered a tight-knit, funny family with all of this energy and camaraderie, and often they reacted to that as much as to our aquariums. Reality TV was just getting off the ground, but everyone used to say: "You guys should really be on television!"

When one or two people tell you something like that, it's a nice compliment, but we kept hearing it more and more frequently, especially once

The tattoo parlor tank

the reality format took off with shows like *Big Brother* and *Survivor*. At first, I just daydreamed about what it would be like to have our family on TV, without really taking the idea seriously. It seemed like a long shot. But the more I thought about it, the more determined I became to make something happen or at least go down swinging.

I tried to get Wayde to take the idea seriously, but with so much to do just to keep ATM afloat he didn't have the time or inclination to get sucked into another one of my "visions." Looking back, I can't blame him for having his doubts. A mountain of work had buried him, and all I wanted to talk about was how we could all be stars. Given my less than exemplary work ethic back then, you can only imagine how many times he told me to quit worrying about getting famous and start selling some tanks instead.

My sister, father, and everyone else in the office knew I might be right about the viability of a show about our family, but they still thought it would never happen. None of us had any experience or contacts in the entertainment industry, so it just seemed like another one of Brett's crazy schemes to get famous. Heck, even *I* felt that way most of the time, which kept me from doing anything about it for a few years.

But then one day Wayde changed his tune. I was pitching him on the idea for the millionth time when he finally snapped and said, "Fine, you don't do anything around here anyway, so just go off and work on this TV show. If it's such a great idea, don't keep bugging me about it. Go make it happen."

Turns out that challenge from Wayde changed all of our lives.

The first person I asked for help was a professor at the University of Nevada at Las Vegas who had a lot of experience in television production. I invited him to tour our office and meet the ATM team. We talked about the different elements that make for a successful reality TV show and what production and development companies want

> "Wayde finally snapped and said, 'Fine, you don't do anything around here anyway, so just go off and work on this TV show. If it's such a great idea, don't keep bugging me about it. Go make it happen.'"

to see before deciding to film a pilot. I hoped the professor would want to shoot it himself as a class project or something, but he didn't have the budget to pull that off. Still, he said we had something special and encouraged me to find a professional production company.

So I opened the Yellow Pages and started dialing. I made hundreds of cold calls, contacting anyone I could find in television and video production, getting nothing but rejection and disappointment in return. But like a shark that's caught the scent of blood in the water, I never stopped pushing for what I wanted. Something told me that getting ATM on TV was how I'd finally realize my dream of being famous.

After more than a year of spinning my wheels, a production company in Los Angeles agreed to shoot some footage of us and edit it into a reel. We all had a lot of fun during those few days of filming, but then the crew went back to LA, and we never heard back from them. I called, and they told me to be patient. A month went by, and they said the same thing. Another month, and still no news. Then they stopped returning my calls entirely, which was heartbreaking. Meanwhile, everyone in the family kept asking what was going on with the TV show, and I didn't know what to tell them. I let myself get so pumped up during that initial filming, but then everybody started treating the idea like some kind of silly fantasy. They used to joke about it.

> "Like a shark that's caught the scent of blood in the water, I never stopped pushing for what I wanted."

I never stopped trying, but all that negativity took its toll on my faith that we would triumph—especially since it came from the people closest to me. At the same time, I've always loved proving people wrong when they doubt or underestimate me, so perhaps that also gave me the extra motivation I needed. After a year, the original production company's contract to produce the show was about to expire, and they wanted to renew. I said no way. If they didn't believe in the project enough to return my phone calls, why should we sign up for more of the same? Instead, I

decided to do something unorthodox. I put our reel in the bottom drawer of my desk and resolved not to touch it for a while.

It's just like meeting a woman, I figured. If you try too hard, hitting the singles bars and spewing out pick-up lines, you're going to get rejected because you sound desperate or you'll get involved with the wrong woman. Even worse, you might miss out on your perfect match when she's standing in line behind you at the supermarket. That was a tough lesson to learn when it came to the TV show, but it turns out I was right. After so much hustling and disappointment, when our big break finally came along, it actually fell right into my lap.

My old college buddy Joel Brown dropped me a line saying that he had just moved to Vegas and wanted to reconnect. By that point, the idea of a reality show had become a sore subject for me around the office, but when Joel asked what I'd been up to lately I decided to fill him in on the whole saga. At the end, he asked to see the sizzle reel, so I pulled it out of the drawer for the first time in six months and popped it in. I left the room while it played so I wouldn't influence his reaction. Thirty minutes later he came busting out of my office and said, "Dude, that's a hit show!"

I've known Joel a long time, and his enthusiasm was 100 percent genuine. For the first time in two years, I felt like someone was on my side. It really lifted my spirits. Then Joel told me that his best friend worked as an executive producer for a television station and he wanted to send him the tape for his professional opinion. His friend turned out to be Mike Skouras, now an executive producer on *Tanked* and the talent agent for the entire cast. Mike took one look at our tape and knew it would be huge if we ever got on television. He couldn't believe that nobody had picked us up earlier. A tremendous sense of relief washed over me. I knew something really big was about to happen. He brought in an industry friend—Nancy Glass, who had her own production company—to shop the idea for the show.

> "Something really big was about to happen."

Nancy Glass Productions recut our sizzle reel to make it more professional. They had a six-month window to sell the project, but it took them

only three weeks to get us a deal. They pitched it to Animal Planet, which was already looking for a new show with an aquatic theme. When the demo tape made its way to Sara Helman, their manager of development at the time, she watched it and then literally ran down the hall to show her boss, Charlie Foley, who had been looking specifically for an aquarium-building business. He watched the reel, and the rest is history. What a feeling—I'll never forget it!

The best part wasn't accomplishing my goal or getting to be on TV, though. It was contributing to the well-being of my family in a way that we can all share and celebrate together. I may have gotten the ball rolling, but every one of us plays a part in what makes *Tanked* a success. That's always been the best part of working with my family, even before the show started. When something funny happens in the office, we're all here. We don't have to go home and explain it. If we make a million-dollar sale, we can all jump up and down together because we're all working on our common dream.

I took a lot of that for granted for too many years, and I'm sorry that I did. Hopefully making *Tanked* a reality makes up for some of that. Wayde still loves to give me a hard time about not working hard enough, but now his jokes are a lot more lighthearted. (Mostly I think he's trying to keep me from getting too big a head.)

We still have our fights, though, just like the family on *American Chopper*, the reality TV hit that first inspired me to push ATM in the direction of themed aquariums. That show followed Paul Teutul Sr. and Jr. of Orange County Choppers in Newburgh, New York, as they made incredible, one-of-a-kind, themed motorcycles. In each episode you see exactly what goes into their manufacturing while a family of big personalities keeps laughing, screaming, crying, fighting, and carrying on. The show always maintained a great balance, and I knew that we could do the same thing with our aquariums for a whole new audience.

In fact, when I was pitching *Tanked* to producers, I used to call it a cross between *American Choppers* and *Married . . . with Children.* And I think that's exactly where we ended up: taking the family comedy from *Married*

. . . with Children and the awesome builds from *American Choppers* and merging them together. You've got close-knit family members who playfully abuse one another but also stick together and work together, making the most mind-blowing custom aquariums imaginable.

Wayde will tell you that I get way too excited about celebrity encounters, but nothing will ever compare to meeting Paul Teutul Sr. at a party thrown by the Discovery Channel, a sister network to Animal Planet. Not only do I love *American Choppers* and respect the work Senior does on those bikes, but the guy seriously changed my life just by showing me what was possible every week on his show. That's why I always take people seriously when they tell me that *Tanked* changed their lives. You never know what's going to help someone through a rough time or open their eyes to some new possibility. I literally used to tell Wayde, "If those guys from Orange County Choppers can do it, why not us?" I made that comparison so many times that it drove him nuts. So imagine how I felt when I finally got the chance to shake Senior's hand and say, "Thanks, man, you're the reason we're on TV."

Nobody had ever built custom-made, elaborately themed aquariums before—in wild shapes and full of props—but watching those guys turn a Harley into a work of art made me believe that we could do the same with a fish tank. We already had all the necessary skills, materials, and machines. All we needed was the creative spark to make it happen, which just so happens to be my specialty. From there, we've never looked back.

> "Not only do I love American Chopper and respect the work Senior does on those bikes, but the guy seriously changed my life just by showing me what was possible every week on his show."

ATM may have created the concept of themed aquariums, but we've been making them only for about four years now, so there're still so many new places to take it. We'll never run out of ideas because what we're doing has elevated the playing field when it comes to aquariums. As Wayde said, we like to call our creations "living art."

The first tank that reflected that shift, for me, was the car aquarium that we built in the pilot episode. Before that, the closest we came to implementing a theme was matching the color of the coral and the lights or putting in a little castle for the fish to swim through. We designed that unforgettable tank for a longtime client named Allen who owned 702 Motoring, a badass high-end custom car shop not far from the ATM office. Allen and his girlfriend, Alese, already had three ATM aquariums in their home, which they loved, so when the car shop was approaching its tenth anniversary, she decided to surprise him with a completely over-the-top tank for their lobby. Then she threw us two major curveballs. She wanted the tank itself to be in the shape of an old hot rod, and she needed it done in two weeks for the car shop's anniversary party.

Typically, from design to installation, it takes us between six and eight weeks to build a custom aquarium of that complexity, so Wayde wasn't exactly thrilled about having to turn it around so quickly. But I knew he would agree because he loves a challenge and hates saying no to a client.

As far as we knew, nobody had cut an automobile in half and turned it into an aquarium before, so we just went for it. The first challenge was finding the right car as quickly as possible because none of the other work could move forward until that happened. I asked around, and luckily the brother of one of our employees had a perfect vehicle that he was already looking to get rid of: a 1957 milk truck. But it wasn't exactly in mint condition. In fact, when I showed up in the ATM parking lot, towing it behind me like something salvaged from the junkyard, Wayde called it a "bucket of crap" and Heather said I was out of my mind. Honestly I thought they were going to say no without even hearing me out.

Fortunately, though, I think that by then they had learned to put a little trust in my visions because they decided to try out my plan—at least once they realized that we didn't have time to find another car . . . and we couldn't get our money back on the one I'd already bought!

First we gutted the old milk truck entirely and stripped it down to its frame. Then we cut it down the middle, lengthwise, so it would sit flush

Telling Robbie how fast we had to complete the hot rod tank

against the wall once installed and built a steel frame to support the weight of an acrylic tank in the shape of the car's windows, with room beneath the frame to store the tank's pump, filter, and life-support system.

Robbie the Redneck nearly fell out of his cowboy hat when he heard how quickly it all needed to come together, but we never doubted that he'd get it done. He just showed up here one day, out of the blue, about fifteen years ago, looking for work. No letter, no phone call, no e-mail, no appointment. He'd cut acrylic and made aquarium inserts for other manufacturers but wanted a new challenge, so we gave him a chance. Now he's among the best in the world at making custom tanks and another member of the family.

In the case of the car aquarium, though, in addition to manufacturing the stand, designing the plumbing, and shaping the acrylic, Robbie also had to transform the inside of the milk truck into something worthy of our favorite custom car shop. He turned the headlight into a little tank with its own adjustable filtration system and converted the gas tank so you can fill the aquarium with water like you would have filled the car with gas. He had a steering wheel and fuzzy dice made to look like coral and outfitted the whole thing with a bunch of colored LED lights linked up to a remote

control. To top it all off, our buddy Marcus Suarez, a world famous graffiti artist, gave the outside of the truck an amazing custom paint job with a giant octopus and yellow sea monsters running down the side. Can you imagine what the milkman who drove it around in the 1950s would have thought about that?!

To source marine life worthy of such a creation, Wayde and I made a special trip to Los Angeles and met with one of our favorite fish suppliers, Exotic Reef Imports. They helped us pick out fish colorful enough to keep up with the truck's wild paint job but passive enough to live together happily in a relatively small space. We started with some beautiful naso fish, sometimes called lipstick fish because of their pronounced fish lips. They do well in a school, so we got five of them. Plus a snowflake eel—among the most peaceful of the morays and a great fit for the trunk tank because they rarely grow over two feet long in captivity. For even more color, we added a blue spotted sharp-nosed puffer and a metallic foxface (even though their dorsal fins are poisonous).

Put it all together, and there's no denying it: We truly made a work of art. But what I love best about that tank is how it reminds me of the rush of excitement I felt to be shooting our first episode of *Tanked,* knowing it would air on Animal Planet and change our lives forever. I can't tell you how proud I was to be part of the ATM team as we all pooled our talents to get the job done on an incredibly tight deadline. Somehow we managed to install the tank *just* in time for the dramatic reveal at the anniversary party.

The reaction from our clients blew us away.

"I've worked really hard for the last ten years," Allen said when he saw his hot rod aquarium for the first time, "so to have my girlfriend surprise me with such an amazing present means the world to me."

Maybe that's where Heather got the idea to surprise Wayde with an octopus tank above his desk (at the old office) for his next birthday. It was shaped like a porthole and fit into the wall between my office and his so we both could look up at it during the middle of a busy workday to feel a little of that famous aquarium tranquility. Which is great because these days, trying to balance being a single dad with the constant demands of a booming business and filming it to boot, I've got to take my relaxation

Prepping the hot rod . . .

The finished hot rod tank

A clandestine shot of me getting some work done through one of the portholes of Wayde's Octopus tank (see page 128)

any way I can get it. Not that I'm complaining—it's just hard sometimes to find time to goof off like I used to.

Animal Planet premiered *Tanked* on a Sunday night in August, but we didn't get to see the finished product until it aired on TV, so I made some special snacks and then sat down on the couch with my kids to watch the first episode just like everyone else . . . except my heart was beating like crazy. I was so excited and more than a little nervous. After all that work to make it happen and pulling my whole family and best friends along for the ride, what if it somehow fell flat? Or I said something dumb enough during the countless hours of filming to turn me into a laughingstock?

But by the first commercial break, a smile spread across my face that felt permanent. I told my kids that from now on things would be different; it was the start of a new era in our lives. We'd always be the same people, and nothing about the way we loved one another would change, but the world was going to look at us a little differently. My daughter was only fourteen at the time, though, and she didn't get it. I'm an excitable guy, and

at first she didn't see much difference between the show and everything else I get all worked up over.

The next morning, though, we went to one of her favorite stores for some back-to-school shopping, and literally the first person we saw when we got out of the car pointed me out to her kids and said, "That's the guy from the fish tank show we watched last night!" The first person we saw inside the store did the same thing. At which point my daughter face-palmed and shook her head. She couldn't believe what was happening. Neither of us could, really, though we're all a lot more used to it now.

Some people complain about "the demands of celebrity," but for me meeting fans has always been a real treat. I especially love hearing from people who watch *Tanked* with their own families, just as I do with my kids, because I think there's precious little on television these days that brings the generations together like that. We're not a cartoon or a kids show, but young people love to see exotic fish, not to mention all the skill and artistry that goes into making our aquariums. Then there're the e-mails we get from Asia, Brazil, Italy, Greece—all over the world. One e-mail came from Malta, a European country just south of Sicily and so small that I had to look it up. It's so cool to correspond with new friends from such distant places and notice the differences, like the way that Germans love reef aquariums and Asians favor freshwater tanks for instance.

Wayde and I both fly internationally a lot these days, and we always arrive at the airport an extra (extra) hour early so we can stop and chat with all the fans we meet going from security to our gate. I can't tell you how many different countries we've been in and had a little crowd form around us, waiting for a picture or an autograph. It's exciting and humbling to realize we're bringing the world of aquariums to millions of people in places we've never been and might never see.

My dream assignment for ATM, however, would be right here in the United States, installing an American history–themed aquarium in the White House. We could call it the First Fish Tank. That would be the ultimate. I mean, I'm all about "Lifestyles of the Fish and Famous,"

right? So who's a bigger star than the leader of the free world?

Over the years, we've built and installed a lot of celebrity tanks, many without even knowing it. Before we were on TV, the big stars just wanted us in and out without any hassle, typically leaving the details for someone else to handle. But now that *Tanked* is a hit, that's changed, and most of our famous clients go out of their way to make sure they have a chance to watch us work. In fact, that's true for pretty much all of our clients now, which is cool because they're usually pretty interesting people and we love getting to know them better so we can make custom tanks that are truly personalized.

> "My dream assignment for ATM would be installing an American history–themed aquarium in the White House."

Tracy Morgan is probably my favorite celebrity for whom we've built a tank since starting the show. He took such a personal interest in his aquarium and wanted to be involved completely with everything we did to make it happen. He hung out with us a lot while we worked, and Wayde and I even slept on his couch and ate what we wanted out of his fridge—like we were old friends working together on a home improvement project. He was the first major star we had on the show, so we definitely didn't expect that. He still calls every once in a while to check in, see how we're doing, and tell us how much he loves his new shark tank.

Stephen Tyler from Aerosmith also calls if he's having an issue with his tank and needs some advice. He actually showed up at our office the first time without any warning, just rode in on his motorcycle and said, "Hey guys, I've heard of you, and I want an awesome aquarium for my house in Hawaii."

Neil Patrick Harris was tremendously fun to work with and a total professional when it comes to being on television. He's a top comedic actor, so it felt great whenever I made him laugh—especially because I wasn't reading lines from a script or planning anything in advance. I was holding my own with him using just my natural wit. Just be yourself around celebrities, and it usually works out fine.

Tracy Morgan treated us like old friends (see page 154).

The craziest celebrity encounter of my life, though, was with James Woods, one of my favorite actors of all time. We met at a party, and *he* asked *me* for a picture to show his grandkids. Here's a true Hollywood icon, somebody whose movies I watched growing up . . . and *he's* running over to get in a photo with Wayde and me? It was all I could do to keep from breaking into my red carpet dance.

That was something I actually came up with long before we even started shooting the pilot for *Tanked.* I used to tell my father, sister, and brother-in-law that we'd all be walking down the red carpet together someday at a big premiere or awards show, so I needed to practice my moves in advance. I danced around, and we'd all have a laugh.

It was a joke, of course, because nobody—not even me—could picture that sort of thing happening way back then. Now, who knows? Stranger things have happened. But even if *Tanked* ends tomorrow, the best and most important aspects of my life would continue uninterrupted. I'd still be a father to my children, I'd still get to make the world's most astounding aquariums, and I'd still get to spend every day working with the people who know me best and love me most. We'll always consider ourselves a family-run aquarium company that just happens to be on television and never the other way around—but I do love that the show allows us to touch people's lives in a positive way. Plus, we get to share everything we know about aquariums and marine life with the world. It's not exactly playing shortstop for the New York Yankees, but, hey, I'll take it!

Brett Raymer
COO, ATM

HEATHER

We've always been a really close-knit family. My father worked from home, so he always made time for us when we needed him. Also, my parents had one of those storybook marriages: They complemented each other perfectly and made everyone around them feel good. They loved to go on vacation together several times a year, taking off for weeks at a stretch, even though it meant making less money. Not that we suffered for it, living in Manhattan Beach, an upscale little peninsula at the bottom of Brooklyn with the Atlantic Ocean to the south and east.

* * *

Growing up, I was really into gymnastics and typical girl stuff like going to the mall and the movies. I also loved to spend time with my siblings, especially my older brother, who in my eyes could do no wrong. "Brett" was actually my first word. Later you might even say he was my idol. I loved his energy, the way he was always getting into everything. I have so many good memories of our childhood. Our younger brother had friends over one day, and I had nothing to keep me occupied, so Brett took me out and said we could do whatever I wanted, all day. We went to the beach, the video arcade, and the rides at Coney Island. On the way back, he bought me my first Cabbage Patch doll.

Sitting on my dad's lap as a toddler

Whenever I had my eye on something that our parents wouldn't get for me, I went straight to him. When I was eight, I wanted a boom box. Mom said no, so Brett bought it for me. By the time I started high school, we were still close, but we weren't spending quite as much time together. It was probably hard for him to see me turning from a little girl into a young woman.

I started community college in Brooklyn, but when my father made the move to his dream home in Las Vegas I followed the family and transferred to UNLV. At first I hated living here. Las Vegas has exploded in size over the last nineteen years, but back then it was like moving to the sticks. I must have flown back to Brooklyn six times that first year to visit Brett and get back to what I'd been missing. If there's one thing I could change about those years, it would be to put more effort into school. I had it pretty easy, so I never really applied myself much. That's the big difference between Wayde and me. He works so hard because of the way he grew up. I really respect that about him—even if sometimes I wish he didn't push himself quite so hard.

My big brother and me

My dad had given me an ultimatum: Either start cracking the books or drop out entirely and work for him. The academic life wasn't right for me, so I took his offer, stopped going to school, and signed on to help run his business. He sold machinery, equipment, and office furniture to government agencies, almost entirely over the phone, which made me hate that job—because I'm a people person and crave face-to-face interaction—but it was good money, so I stuck it out.

I was sitting there one day, going over bidder lists for some contract, when in walks Wayde to work on the aquarium he was building for our family. He'd already gotten in good with my mother and had even tried to get her to set the two of us up based on a picture of me he saw hanging in the living room. No dice, though, because I'd moved to Nevada with my boyfriend from New York, and we were still an item. Not that that discouraged Wayde in the least. He kept making up excuses to visit the house just to see me, and slowly we struck up a friendship.

One afternoon I found myself confiding in him that it wasn't working out with my boyfriend, and we were going to split up. That's when Wayde told me, point blank, that he was going to make me his wife. Such a direct approach really took me aback. I didn't take him seriously at first, but obviously seventeen years later he's a man of his word!

As you can see on the show, Wayde has a tough, burly exterior, but he also has a huge heart. The way

> "Wayde told me, point blank, that he was going to make me his wife."

he strived so hard to achieve his goals made him really attractive to me. On some of our earliest dates I just went to a job site and kept him company while he laid tiles or did other contracting work. It's mind boggling how many different skills he's mastered. To see him apply that much knowledge was a big turn-on, especially when he's so passionate about whatever he does. You don't find that quality in a lot of people these days.

It got serious between us pretty quickly. Once we started our romance, I couldn't remember a time when we weren't together. We had the same dreams and desires. I wanted to get married young and start having

Wayde and I on our big day

children, so it worked perfectly—and it still works. I mean, you may see us argue on TV and think otherwise, but anybody who tells you they've got the perfect relationship and they never fight is lying. We've had our ups and downs, but we're still standing side by side, which really says something.

Right around the time we got engaged, Brett moved from Brooklyn to Las Vegas so our whole family could be together. That thrilled me—except for one problem. Brett and Wayde didn't see eye-to-eye . . . particularly when it came to me. As you can imagine, that put yours truly in a difficult position, especially once we all went into business together, just months before my wedding.

By the time Wayde and I went to Hawaii on our honeymoon, I'd started to help out at ATM on a regular basis, including a lot of hands-on research

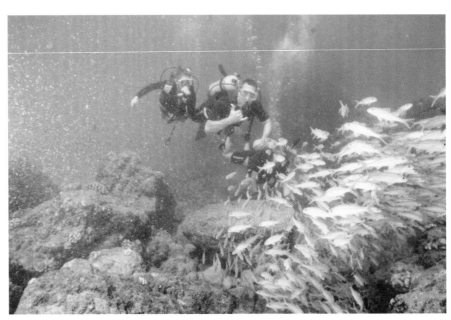

Snorkeling on our honeymoon

and investigation into the world of aquariums. When we went scuba diving as part of a tour of the islands, I loved it and discovered that I already could identify many of the fish we saw. Today my favorite fish in our home tanks are the puffers and parrot fish, which remind me of the ones we saw together in Hawaii.

When we got back home, interacting with our customers quickly became my favorite part of the fish tank business, and it still is. Clients

> "Brett and Wayde didn't see eye-to-eye . . . particularly when it came to me."

and suppliers who come to the shop get a huge kick out of our different personalities. We were the same then as we are now. We're not actors, we can't fake anything. What you see is what you get: the good, the bad, our lives. Like Brett says, everybody kept telling us that we should be on TV. People say that a lot, but in this case they were right, and my brother gets a lot of credit for realizing that and following his dream. Otherwise, *Tanked*

never would have happened, the same way that ATM never would have happened without all of Wayde's hard work and my father's willingness to take a chance on my new husband and me.

After Wayde and I had been married for about two years, my mother was diagnosed with cancer. The doctors didn't give her long to live, and Wayde and I had already been discussing having a baby. With my mother's condition looking precarious, we decided to move forward immediately to give her a chance to see her first grandchild. In the meantime, my father closed up his business, allowing us both to spend as much time caring for her as possible. Wayde had to work even harder at ATM, but he did it so I could focus on what was really important to me, and I can't ever thank him enough for that.

The morning that my water broke, I was at home with my mother. She was going through chemotherapy at the time, so she wanted to put on her eyebrows and makeup before we left the house, which took quite a while. We lived only a few minutes from the hospital, but all I could think was: *Wayde's going to get there before we do and freak out.* He was a nervous wreck about the birth. Don't get me wrong, Wayde's great under pressure and does whatever needs doing, but he gets this look on his face sometimes that shows a little of the panic behind his usual commanding presence. (Don't tell him that I told you, but he actually threw up from nerves right after our wedding ceremony!)

It turns out, though, that I was in labor for nearly twelve hours. The whole event turned into a crazy kind of party. Wayde never left my side.

His mother was also there, and at one point she very sweetly took my mother into the bathroom and shaved her head for her so her wig would fit better. My father never once stopped pacing. Meanwhile, I wasn't allowed to have any food or beverages . . . but they were all chugging Starbucks! I'll never forget, though, when my first daughter finally came into the

world and they handed her to me. My mother looked down at her sweet little face and said, "Oh Heather, she's beautiful!"

Even though she's gone now, when I close my eyes, I can still hear my mother saying those words, and I love knowing that Wayde and I could give her that gift at the end of her life. From that moment, I've tried to be as good a mother to my kids as she was to me. I miss her so much, and I wish my daughters could have gotten to know her, but I will always have that one precious memory of us together.

After that, I took a hiatus from ATM to focus on being a stay-at-home mom. I sometimes helped out around the office when it got busy, but I didn't come in much from then until the economy tanked in 2008 and we faced a real crisis just keeping the business going. That was an incredibly difficult, stressful time—particularly when we had to lay people off—but it gave us the opportunity to pull closer together as a family. With our backs to the wall, we learned a lot about ourselves and how much we really depend on one another, especially Brett and Wayde, who stopped focusing on each other's weaknesses and began to work better together as a team.

The best example of that change is *Tanked*. Brett used to obsess about getting our own TV show, and Wayde always told him to stop dreaming and get back to work. But either Wayde got totally fed up or he had a "vision" of his own because he finally realized that Brett works really hard only when he's chasing one of his own dreams. Wayde challenged him to work on getting the company on TV, which inspired Brett to stop talking about it and make a plan.

It started with a small film crew who came into our old office hoping to shoot just enough footage to sell the idea to someone else. I wasn't meant to be a part of the show, but I kind of got thrown into the mix. It didn't for one second occur to me that it was going to lead to a hit series, so I never really worried about it. But once I knew we were going to have our own show, I started to get apprehensive. It all sounded great in theory—it would help the business and we'd enjoy some notoriety—but how would

it affect my family? Wayde and I have always been private people. We have very outgoing personalities, sure, but mostly we like to spend time among our closest friends and family. The idea that our lives would be broadcast all over the world took getting used to.

One point that helped me decide to go for it was knowing that we would be part of a high-quality program with an educational aspect that's appropriate for family viewing. Don't get me wrong, I love trashy reality TV—all of the housewives and Kardashians—but I didn't want to take my own family in that direction. It's really gratifying that our show doesn't focus on the negative. Sure, you catch us bickering or stressing out from time to time, but we're always working together toward the same shared goal, and it all comes from a place of love and mutual respect—even when we're playing pranks on one another. Or maybe I should say *especially* when we're playing pranks on one another. Remember: We never knowingly do something that's going to be mean or hurtful to each other.

One of the best pranks that Brett and Wayde played on me appeared in the first episode of the show. They were working on a nice aquarium at the Palms Casino, right here in Las Vegas, and they needed my help because the design for the coral inserts called for putting them in a small space that neither of them could access. I'm certified for scuba diving and only 5 feet tall, so, after some serious convincing, I agreed to help them out. The work had to be done that day, so we went straight to the casino. Only, when we arrived, there'd been some kind of mix-up, and the tank already had about *twenty* sharks in it, including a black-tip that looked capable of tearing me in two with one snap of its jaws!

> "I was absolutely petrified, way more frightened than I've ever been before or since."

Between facing my fear of being eaten alive, dealing with a bunch of cameras that I wasn't used to, and knowing that a million people around the world (including my daughters) would end up seeing whatever happened—I was absolutely petrified, way more frightened than I've ever been before or since. To calm me down, my husband and my brother assured me that we

Wayde and I enjoy a moment of fun with our daughters, Taylor and Morgan.

all would have special "shark sticks" to protect us. The sticks felt more like toothpicks, but somehow I got through it. When it was all over, I felt really proud of myself not just for facing my fears but for helping Wayde. I wasn't even mad at him for putting me in that situation . . . until the show aired later and I found out that there's no such thing as a "shark stick." They were just mop handles!

> "There's no such thing as a 'shark stick.' They were just mop handles!"

Believe it or not, Wayde and I don't get to see the show until it airs. Our girls are usually at gymnastics practice on Friday nights, so we DVR it and watch together as a family once they get home. It was hard to see myself on TV at first—it's easy to be self-critical—but I've really come to love the show. Among other things, it's a professionally produced home movie of our lives that we'll have forever. Meanwhile, my kids' favorite part is always the fish facts. They take after Wayde in being very into all kinds of animals. For the last two summers, instead of going to sleep-away camp, our daughters decided to spend their time at ATM instead. We've found them all kinds of jobs, mostly helping to care for the animals, which is their main interest in the business at this point. They also take care of our koi pond and aquarium at home too.

Sometimes watching *Tanked* can prove frustrating because they tape so much more than they possibly can squeeze into each episode. You wonder what happened to this or that. At the same time, I naturally don't see everything that happens with Wayde, Brett, and my dad, so sometimes one of them will make a joke and I'll laugh like crazy just like anyone else.

None of us felt at ease on camera initially. The first green screens for the show were done at my house. That's when they set you up in front of a special background and then ask you questions about something that happened. You rephrase their questions and then answer them, which felt so uncomfortable to me. I worried about every word I said as it came out of my mouth. But once I got used to the process and the crew, that quickly changed. It no longer feels like strangers are following me around with a camera. We've all become friendly, so it's much easier—and I can do green screens in a snap now!

People sometimes ask what it's like to be a "star," but I don't know because I don't perceive myself that way. When it comes to *Tanked,* I'm just being myself and letting people watch. The only real stars on our show are the amazing aquariums that we build. For me, being on television pales in comparison to the excitement of watching my kids grow up. My first job is and always will be as a mom. So whenever a fan asks for an autograph or

wants to say hello, it always feels a little surreal—like they must have me confused with someone else. But knowing that five minutes of my time could make a child's whole day . . . I mean, even *adults* have gotten teary-eyed, which boggles my mind because I've never easily been star-struck.

It does makes me realize, though, that they feel a deep connection to our show and therefore to our family. We're bringing something positive into their lives, and they want to say thank you, which is genuinely humbling. That's why, when the tour buses come to visit the ATM facility, Wayde and I go out to the retail store to greet them. Once fans meet us and see that we're just the same as on the show, they love it. They come from all over the world, most of them families just like us. They all watch the show together, and many say that we've inspired them to set up their own tanks to take care of and enjoy.

People like aquariums because they're soothing and beautiful to look at, and these days everybody needs something to take them to that tranquil place. ATM brings it to a whole new level by building these living pieces of art, so you've got both the wow factor and the tranquillity. We can also make something incredibly personal that reflects the home of the family where it will reside.

If I had to name one frustration, it's that the limitations of television sometimes make it look like Wayde doesn't spend enough time with me or that he forgets that he has family obligations. You don't always see the whole picture. My husband's hard work makes it possible for me to focus 100 percent on our daughters. At one point, when I was working full time, taking care of the kids, and filming the show all at once, he said to me: "Who do you think you are, Superwoman?" Well, yeah, in my own way I did, but I was wrong. I couldn't do it all.

Would I like Wayde to spend more time with me? Of course. Who wouldn't want that with the person they love most? But he's providing for me and our daughters, and I've never missed a gymnastics meet or a school function, thanks to him. Everything in life is give and take. That doesn't always come across on the show, but there are only so many hours in the day. We've been together seventeen years, and it's still a learning process—as it should be. The biggest lesson we've learned is to keep everything in perspective. Wayde doesn't like to be questioned at work, and I don't like to be questioned at home. So how do we separate what happens at work from what happens at home? It's difficult sometimes, but I understand him so well that I can anticipate his needs better than anyone else, and I (usually) know how to avoid pissing him off. Plus, you can't fire your family, so what's he gonna do?

Heather King
Co-owner and Accounting, ATM

IRWIN "THE GENERAL"

I was born on November 22, 1944, or 11/22/44, an extremely auspicious date in numerology that predicted a life of great accomplishment.

• • •

My parents divorced when I was very young—almost unheard of at the time—so my mother and I moved in with my grandparents in Brooklyn, New York, where we shared an 81-square-foot room with two beds, a chest of drawers, and a steam pipe. When I was twelve, my mother remarried, and we moved to a new apartment not much bigger. I grew up there, poor but happy, playing basketball and running track at Fort Hamilton High School, where I graduated in 1962. For you younger viewers or readers, that was the year that the Beatles released their first record, *West Side Story* won best picture at the Oscars, and John F. Kennedy occupied the White House. A gallon of gasoline cost 31 cents, and a cup of coffee cost a dime.

At Long Island University, I tried out for the basketball team. The coach liked my hustle so much that he approved me for a scholarship, but, when I took the physical required to qualify, they discovered a hernia, and I lost the scholarship. So I dropped out of school to focus on making money. My uncle helped me find work at a sweatshop on Union Street in Brooklyn, earning $65 per week as part of the old New York garment industry that's now gone mostly overseas. We made sportswear in a cramped factory space with no air conditioning. Compared to going to college and shootings hoops, it wasn't much fun, but I hung tough and learned the trade from the ground up.

Before long, the boss had me supervising more than fifty guys, most of them much older than I was. I learned how to organize the payroll and suggested improvements that saved the company a lot of money. I worked

Looking sharp as always

there only a year, but it was a great education. By the end, the boss trusted me enough to put me in charge while he took his first vacation in ten years. He treated me with a lot of respect, even though I was so young, which meant a lot to me. It was hard to leave when the time came, but I didn't want to work in a sweatshop forever.

In 1967 I joined the NYPD and served on the force for the next fifteen years. It was a turbulent time in our nation's history, nowhere more so than in New York City. I spent my entire law enforcement career there as a patrolman, walking a beat. That taught me to rely on my instincts and how to size people up. I like to say that my logic will outdo your knowledge because anything you can read in a book I can read in the same book, but the kind of street smarts I absorbed while twirling my nightstick along the back alleys of Gotham aren't so easy to obtain.

I'd also rather work smarter than harder. Long before *Tanked,* people used to ask me how I made my fortune after growing up with nothing. Well, I did it by being smarter than everybody else. Maybe that sounds conceited, but it's not like I invented the light bulb. I just saw opportunities other people overlooked and figured out how to make myself a bundle.

That's how I got into the discount machinery and equipment business. I started small, while still on the force, but quickly realized how much money I could earn simply by making the necessary phone calls to supply my clients' needs. Opportunities exist like that in all kinds of industries. The hard part isn't taking advantage of them, it's finding them. Some day I'm going to write a book called *Why Am I Always Right?* so I can teach what I know to the rest of the world. A book like that certainly could have saved my son and son-in-law a lot of headaches back when we started ATM.

Eventually I earned enough to take early retirement from the force at age forty and work at the supply business just twelve hours per week, from home. My wife and I went on vacation for eighteen weeks every year, visiting the Caribbean, South America, Europe, Africa, Asia, Australia—anywhere and everywhere we ever wanted to go.

> "My logic will outdo your knowledge."

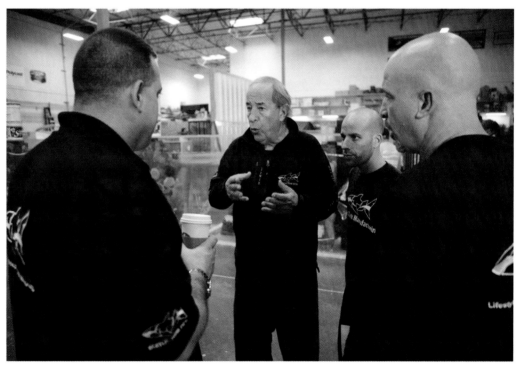

Explaining my logic and why I'm right, yet again, to Wayde, Frankie, and Brett

Sure, I could have worked more and made even more money, but I decided to focus on enjoying what I already had, rather than getting caught up in the never-ending struggle for power and influence. Bill Gates didn't do that; Donald Trump didn't do that. When I think back on all the amazing memories of traveling the world with my wife, I know that keeping a proper balance between labor and leisure was the smartest thing I ever did.

In 1994, after living my entire life in New York City, I fell in love with Las Vegas and decided to build my wife her dream home here. We'd never undertaken a construction project like that before, but we wanted to oversee the whole thing ourselves because this was going to be the last place we lived. It needed to be perfect. A lot of people who come to ATM feel the same way about their aquariums. They want something really personal. To borrow one of Brett's favorite words, you could say I had a "vision" of how I wanted the house to look and feel. To get it done right I had to do it myself, and I knew it would be a fun new challenge.

Acid wash denim in the summer of '88, baby!

All told, it's 12,000 square feet, including a pool, exercise room, and screening room, and I still live there today. It took two full years to construct. My wife and I were like kids in a candy store, making sure everything came out exactly how we wanted. We used to have a small aquarium in our house when our children were young, so I decided to install one in the new place that also functioned as a kind of underwater window between the living room and dining room. I wanted to look through it from one room to the other, which meant finding a custom tank manufacturer to install it while the house was still under construction.

As it turns out, I hired the company where Wayde worked just before they went bankrupt. They had to cancel my contract midway though, but then this young guy from their shop approached me and offered to finish the job himself for the right price. We were still basically strangers at that

point, but my future son-in-law really impressed me with that move. He wasn't undercutting his boss—they were already out of business—but I got a great deal and he earned more building it as an independent contractor than he would have by working for someone else.

He didn't have anywhere else to do the manufacturing, so I let him set up in the garage. Well, one day Wayde notices a photo of my daughter Heather on the wall, and a flash comes over him that they're going to fall in love and get married. Lucky for him, I happen to believe in that kind of intuition. On a fine sunny day, I met my first wife when I was standing in front of Nathan's Famous Hot Dogs in Coney Island in my policeman's uniform. She came up to me, and we talked for a while before exchanging phone numbers. That night she told her mother that she'd just met the man she was going to marry! Naturally our story was floating in the back of my mind when Wayde later explained his own love at first sight.

> "This young guy from their shop approached me and offered to finish the job himself for the right price."

But it was more than intuition that convinced me to help him buy the bankrupt company where he used to work and relaunch it as ATM. I saw the upside potential in the aquarium business and trusted Wayde to do well in it, but on the other hand I also considered myself retired, ready for my money to work for me instead of the other way around. So what

The tank that Wayde built that started it all

changed my mind? A chance to help my daughter and her new husband pursue their dreams together. Working with Wayde has been a long and hard adventure but very successful.

No regrets there, especially now that we've come out on top, but my one big mistake was not keeping close enough watch over my investment during those first few years. I made Brett the president of the company to keep an eye on things, and he's a bright guy, but because of their ages neither he nor Wayde has my business-world experience. As a result, we endured some costly mistakes back then that I probably could have prevented if I'd been involved more directly. My grandfather gave me these words of wisdom when I was young: "Learn from other people's mistakes instead of your own, and you'll save a lot of time, money, and aggravation."

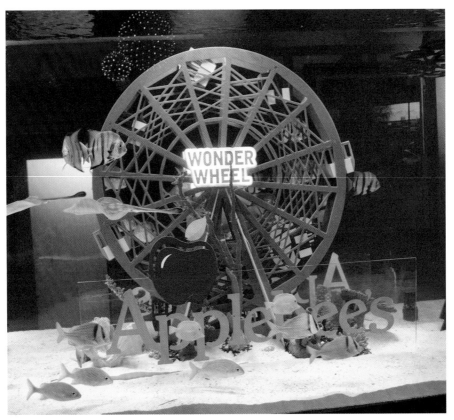

The Wonder Wheel feature from the Coney Island Applebee's tank. That job brought back a lot of memories.

Having a laugh with my kids

In 2008, I was asked out of retirement to help with the business. We'd just caught a former employee embezzling from us, which hurt everyone both financially and personally. Also, in the endless struggle to produce amazingly high-quality aquariums on such tight deadlines, a lot of the bookkeeping needed attention. So I rolled up my sleeves and dug in. I thought it would take a few months and then I could go back to retirement, but now, between working almost full-time at ATM and an intense filming schedule for *Tanked,* I haven't been able to get away for a vacation in more than three years! (We work until 8 p.m. on many occasions.)

I'm actually working harder than I ever have in my life, but the results prove that it's been worth the sacrifice. ATM not only survived the early growing pains, but we weathered the 2008 financial crisis. Of course, I had to invest even more money into the business to get us through the worst of it, but what else could I do? I could have cut my losses and let everyone fend for themselves in those shark-infested waters, but, when you're doing business with family, family comes first.

Brett will probably tell you that *Tanked* saved the company. Sometimes he needs reminding that there would have been nothing left to save if I hadn't floated the business through its darkest days. We basically had landed back on our feet before the first episode ever aired, but, still, I'm really proud of that kid for making his dream happen after all of these years. It's no secret that I pushed him into the aquarium business when he didn't know anything about it, so for him to turn it into something so completely in line with his own "vision" proves what I've always believed: Anything's possible if you know how to apply the right amount of pressure in the right place and at the right time.

> "When you're doing business with family, family comes first."

When Brett first started talking about a reality show about ATM, I'm sure that I laughed at him a little. You have to understand, though: He's been dreaming up schemes to become famous since grade school. This time, he really applied himself, though, and the results speak for themselves.

I enjoy being on the show and getting to meet our wonderful fans, but *Tanked* is important to me mostly because it's important to my family. I had a great life and plenty of money before I made it onto television, and that wouldn't change if they pull the plug on the series tomorrow. I just try to enjoy the whole experience for what it is without worrying about where it might lead or what happens when it's over.

In the meantime, being a part of a show that families sit down together to enjoy really touches my heart. Family is the most important thing in the world to me, and it always will be.

Irwin Raymer
CFO, ATM

The Original Raymer Family Feud

We never aspired to be actors, and none of us so much as tried out for the high school play, but we did enjoy a brief encounter with the bright lights of showbiz long before the show. Fans of *Extreme Home Makeover* may remember Brett from an episode in which a little girl with a serious illness wanted a fish-themed bedroom, and Heather boogied for the cameras on *Dance Party USA* as a teen. Even Wayde got in on the action when he appeared on *Monster Garage* to help Jesse James convert an armored car into a dunk tank.

Wayde recalls: "It was all new to me, and at the time it was one of the most difficult things I'd done. We had to plasma-cut the armored car, weld it, put panels in, and silicon it—all on the work site. Luckily, there was a hot looking girl there with tattoos and a plasma cutter, who was amazing. Another guy was a whiz with robotic arms, so he went in and did all that kind of work. There was even an armored truck specialist. Meanwhile, I did the welding and ended up burning my retinas. I couldn't see the next day."

But none of that compares to the Raymer family's ill-fated appearance on *Family Feud*. For Brett, just out of college then, the chance to appear on one of America's best-loved and longest-running game shows felt like the call of destiny, the first step on his long-awaited journey to fame and fortune. Only, as he explains, it didn't quite work out according to his plan—despite serious practice and preparation.

"My dad thinks he's always right and knows everything about everything," says Brett. "He wants to write a book called *Why Am I Always Right?* To which I say: You weren't right that day on *Family Feud* when you got four wrong answers and cost us the five-thousand-dollar prize!"

It all started when we found out that we were finally making it on the show after five or six tryouts. Right away, we had our friends

come to the house to play the home version of the game and help us train for the real deal. The General served as the head of the team . . . and he was the *worst.* He was so bad over the course of weeks and weeks of practicing that we literally made him sign a waiver that he wasn't going to go out on his own at the end and overrule everybody else's guess.

Naturally, when we were on the show, it all came down to the last question. Keep in mind, the General hadn't gotten a single answer right all day. The final question was: Name something in the house that creaks. Floor, windows, and stairs were all taken, and we had one blank left. If we got it right, we won; if we missed, we went home empty handed.

We huddled up for our final answer, and Brett came up with rocking chair. Everybody in the family agreed, and we were all screaming "Rocking chair!"—but then the General steps up to the microphone and says: "I promised my family I wasn't going to do this, but I'm going to have to go out on my own and say the roof."

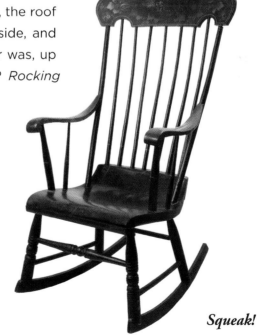

Last time we all checked, the roof is *outside* the house, not inside, and guess what the right answer was, up on the big board. Give up? *Rocking chair!*

On the ride home, we were all bawling our eyes out. We still give him a hard time about it. We might put on his headstone: I WAS WRONG ON *FAMILY FEUD*.

Squeak!

ROBBIE "THE REDNECK"

People have been calling me a redneck almost my entire life, and I always take it as a compliment. If you go and research the history of the term, it actually came from the old shipyards. It's what they used to call guys bent over in the sun all day building the big sailing ships, on account of the perpetual sunburns on the backs of their necks. So really, we're talking about hardworking craftsmen, the kind of guys who get the job done. Nowadays the word has other connotations, some of them kinda negative, but to me it's something to be proud of and celebrate. That's how Wayde and Brett intended it when they gave me the nickname not long after I started working at ATM. We like to bust each other's chops an awful lot, but always from a place of mutual respect. Same way I don't mean nothing by it when I call them a couple of New York City boys.

* * *

As for me, I was born in Rock Springs, Wyoming, and raised all over western Colorado. My family moved around quite frequently on account of my father's job with the Bureau of Reclamation, a federal agency under the US Department of the Interior that brings water to millions of people and huge stretches of farmland throughout the American West. Dad

worked as a construction inspector, so every few years he'd get assigned to a new project and we'd have to pick up and move.

Mostly we lived in small country towns or rural farmland. That kind of upbringing taught me a lot, including how to adjust quickly and adapt to just about anyone or anything thrown at you. Moving around so much also makes you focus on what you can keep constant because everything else inevitably changes. A big part of that for me was making things with my hands whenever possible, an especially important skill out in the country. Before you could order junk on the Internet, either you made it or made do, as the saying goes.

Growing up, I loved hunting, fishing, and anything else having to do with nature and the outdoors. For pets, we had Siamese cats, small dogs, and a freshwater aquarium with angel fish, guppies, and tetras. I used to like sitting in front of it, watching everything going on inside. I guess that aquarium relaxed me, but I never really paid it much mind. I certainly never thought fish tanks would become such a big part of my life. That happened by accident a ways down the road.

I graduated from high school in Grand Junction, Colorado, a year early with a GED. I'd already started working at an amusement park called Guyton's Fun Junction during the summers, operating carnival rides like the Ferris wheel, Tilt-a-Whirl, bumper boats, that sort of thing. Later I learned how to help maintain and repair the rides, which inspired me to enroll at a local trade school and study electronics. To pay for tuition and keep myself afloat, I juggled two jobs. During the day, I worked for a company that manufactured industrial equipment used in the mining industry. At night I cooked at and managed a Mexican restaurant. I was young, with no experience in a commercial kitchen, but I knew how to cook. They gave me a shot.

My favorite dish from the restaurant is one I still make at home today. We called it Indian bread, and it's simple but delicious, my favorite kind of cooking.

ROBBIE'S INDIAN FRY BREAD

Cuisine: Southwest

Prep time: 15 min

Cook time: 8 min

Yield: 4 servings

Fry bread is wonderfully lumpy and can be served a main-dish bread or dessert. My family often stuffs them, the way you might use bread or a tortilla to dip into your food.

1 cup unbleached flour	**1 teaspoon baking powder**
¼ teaspoon salt	**½ cup water**
1 teaspoon powdered milk	**Vegetable oil for frying**

In a large bowl, sift together the flour, salt, powdered milk, and baking powder. Add the water all at once and stir with a fork until the dough starts to form one big clump. With well-floured hands mix the dough, trying to get all the flour into the mixture to form a ball. Do *not* knead it. (Kneading it will make the fry bread too heavy when cooked.) The inside of the dough ball should still be sticky after it's formed, and the outside well floured. Cut the dough into four pieces. Using floured hands, form disks of about 5 to 7 inches in diameter. They don't need to be round.

In a large cast-iron skillet or other large, heavy pot, add enough vegetable oil to fill it 1 inch deep and heat it to about 350°F. (You can check if the oil is hot enough either by dropping in a small piece of dough and seeing if it begins to fry or by dipping in the end of a wooden spoon and seeing if that bubbles.) Gently place the formed dough into the oil, taking care not to splatter the hot oil. Press down on the dough as it fries so the top is submerged. Fry until brown, then flip to fry the other side. Each side will take approximately 3 to 4 minutes to cook. Place the cooked bread on a paper towel to absorb excess oil.

You can keep Indian Fry Bread warm in a 200°F oven for up to an hour. It refrigerates well and can be reheated in a 350°F oven for 10 to 15 minutes before serving.

INDIAN TACOS

Prep time: 15 min

Cook time: 10 min

Yields: 4 servings

Indian Fry Bread serves as the foundation of a popular dish called Indian Tacos, originally known as Navajo Tacos, but adopted by other tribes.

1 pound lean ground meat (beef, lamb, venison, or pork)

1 cup diced onion

4 cooked Indian Fry Breads (see recipe above)

1 head iceberg lettuce, shredded

3 tomatoes, diced

2 cups shredded sharp cheddar cheese

1 (3-ounce) can diced green chiles, drained

Sour cream (optional)

In a large frying pan over medium-high heat, brown ground meat and onions until cooked and remove from heat. Place each Fry Bread, cupped side up, on a plate. Layer ground meat, lettuce, tomatoes, cheese, and chiles onto each. Top with sour cream if you like, and either roll them up or serve open-faced with a fork.

I enjoyed that job, but working while going to school started to burn me out, so I had to quit the kitchen and focus on manufacturing, my true love. I've always been good with my mind and hands, so it's the perfect fit. As long as I can remember, I've always been making or fixing something. I usually can understand how things go together just by looking at them. I might need to glance at a manual for reference points and proper procedures, but as far as taking things apart and putting them back together, I've never needed any instruction. It just comes naturally.

Around this time, I came up with a plan to make some money in the fish business. I had just moved out on my own and decorated my new bachelor pad by setting up a 55-gallon glass aquarium for fancy tailed guppies. Well, I started with six pair—three males and three females—and right away they began making babies. Pretty soon I had more fancy tailed guppies than I knew what to do with—until a local pet store offered to buy them off me. Now, those guppies didn't pay the bills, but even a little extra money went a long way in those days. And who knows? Maybe that's what planted the seed that eventually led me to ATM.

Unfortunately I had to make an unpleasant pit stop along the way. When I was young and wild, I got into fast cars, which led me to drag racing . . . the illegal kind. I got caught and lost my driver's license, but that didn't stop me. Then I got caught again. A judge sent me to prison for a little while to think about what I'd done and how I would have felt if anybody had gotten hurt because of it. That proved more than enough to put me on the straight and narrow from the moment they let me go.

I wasn't incarcerated for long, but I had to make a fresh start afterward. In 1987, I applied for a job with a Grand Junction company that manufactured acrylic. They hired me on a ninety-day probationary period, starting with sanding and polishing acrylic, the lowest job on the totem pole. By the thirty-day mark, they had me managing that department. After sixty days, I moved up to bonding. At the end of ninety days, they made me assistant manager. I climbed the ladder really quickly. That job kept me on the road all the

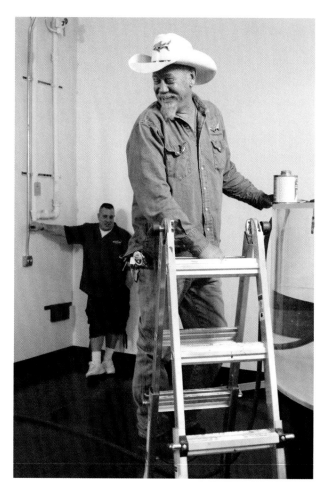

time, for ten years, even after I got married and had kids. Then my wife went back to school and needed to go to Denver and take her final exams. I put in for vacation time to stay home and watch our children—which seemed like the least I could do after three years of traveling back and forth to Canada on a huge project—and I was really looking forward to quality time with the kids.

My boss approved the time off weeks in advance, but three days into it he called to tell me that I had to get on the next flight to Canada.

"I can't," I said.

"If you don't go, you'll be out of a job," he replied.

"Then I guess I don't have a job," I said.

I'm a man of principle, but it wasn't an easy move to make. It was one of the best decisions of my life, but at the time it made me feel terrible.

I took some construction jobs around Colorado to pay the bills but didn't much enjoy the work. On a whim, my wife and I decided to move to Las Vegas. We'd visited many a time on vacation and always had fun, so we had some idea what it would be like. Plus, it was the fastest-growing city in America at the time, which meant I'd have no trouble finding employment in a wide variety of fields.

For the first six months, I did manufacturing jobs for a place that specialized in making artificial rock and coral structures. That's where I heard about a new aquarium manufacturer opening up in town. I missed working

with acrylic, so I headed over to ATM's first office and spent a couple hours talking with Wayde, giving him a rundown of my skills and experience. At the end of our chat, he told me to give my employer notice because I was going to work full time for him.

Wayde and I come from very different backgrounds, but it was obvious right away that we have the same mindset when it comes to what's important, like working hard and focusing on craftsmanship. We also communicated very well, so we naturally clicked. No doubt moving around so much as a kid helped me adjust quickly to working with a bunch of loud New Yorkers—not just Wayde but Brett, Heather, and Irwin, too.

> "At the end of our chat, Wayde told me to give notice because I was going to work full time for him."

They've all treated me pretty much like family from the get go and not just at work or on the job. They've always welcomed me into their home, and we hang out off the clock, too. What you see on television really does reflect how we all get along. You might catch us arguing, but you'll never see anything from the outside come between us. That's an important value we all share, whether learned out in the country or in a huge metropolis. We've formed a tight bond over the years, and that's a big part of why people love the show and identify with what we all go through trying to do our jobs.

Of course, I hope the biggest draw is the high quality of the aquariums we manufacture. That's what makes us different from every other workplace where people joke around and have fun. I'll never forget the first big custom project I worked on at ATM. It was a 12-foot-tall, 3,200-gallon, 10,000-pound saltwater showstopper for a public library in Sarasota, Florida. This was back in 1999, when ATM only had a handful of employees. Wayde and I both went out to pretty much every one of our install

jobs. Only this time, when we got to Sarasota, it felt like the whole city was talking about our aquarium. The local paper had been writing about it for weeks, getting everyone excited.

Well, we had just two days for the installation, which started with a lot of headaches getting a tank that big inside the building. But when we were done, just before the public unveiling, I looked up at what we'd created: a breathtaking arch tank under which patrons would walk when going from the main stacks into the children's section. It was a real work of art and an amazing feeling.

> "Whenever I can transform someone's dream into a fish tank I'm happy."

We've made literally thousands of tanks since, and fans always want to know which one's my favorite. I can't give a proper answer, though, because they're all unique and special to me in one way or another. Whenever I can transform someone's dream into a fish tank I'm happy because I've succeeded in my challenge. That's what's important to me—much more than being on television.

I like to watch nature shows and do-it-yourself shows, but I never thought I'd end up in front of a camera on a show that combines the two. Now that it's happened, I really enjoy the chance to educate and, to a certain extent, entertain, but I don't ever want *Tanked* to change me or my life. I'll just continue being myself and let the chips fall where they may. If you like that, that's great—because I really couldn't do it any other way.

Robert Christlieb
Marine Technician, ATM

AGNES

My life began in Czestochowa, a small town in southern Poland. When I was six years old, my parents immigrated to America to escape the communist dictatorship that controlled our home country. We could move only after my father obtained a special kind of refugee status with the help of our church. The rest of our extended family had to stay behind, though fortunately I visited throughout my childhood, usually to spend the summer. As a result, my Polish roots have always remained strong. I speak the language fluently and cook a mean pierogi.

• • • •

But Las Vegas will always be home. This is where I settled with my parents, and I've never left for long. When we first arrived, however, I couldn't speak ten words in English, and everything seemed so incredibly different from what we'd left behind. The first few weeks, I came home from school crying my eyes out because every word my teacher and classmates said sounded like gibberish. It was even tougher for my brother because he was twelve and kids that age can be really cruel if you're different. But somehow we both got through it.

By second grade, just a year later, I'd learned English almost perfectly. It's amazing to realize what a tremendous gift for picking up new languages we have when we're children. From then on, I did quite well in school. After graduation I enrolled at the University of Nevada at Reno

and majored in optometry, but I had to drop out before graduation to help my mother through a divorce. My parents endured so much to give me and my brother the best life possible, so there was no question. I would do anything for either of them in return.

To keep my days free so I could help my mother, while still making some money, I (stereotypically) took work as a cocktail waitress at some of the big hotels like Mandalay Bay, the Venetian, and the Palms. I was barely old enough to drink, so the glitz and glamour appealed to me. I met a lot of interesting characters in the course of a night's work, but I never wanted to grow old as a cocktail waitress.

Instead, when the chance came along, I attended cosmetology school and then worked as a hairdresser for the next six years. I loved that job in many ways, but I like the idea of a new challenge. When a long-term relationship didn't work out, I took it as an opportunity to make a new beginning. I didn't have a specific plan in mind; I just kept my eyes open, waiting for the right opportunity to come along and find me.

Then, one day I picked up a local Las Vegas magazine to kill some time between appointments at the salon and came across an article about a girl who sold Lamborghinis. I read the article two or three times in one sitting and thought to myself: *Dang, that's off the wall and sounds really cool! That's the kind of job I need!*

The Lamborghini dealer already had a salesgirl on staff, though, so I found the closest Ferrari dealership, drove straight there on a whim, and told the owner upfront that I didn't have any experience selling sports cars. He still agreed to give me a chance because I took the initiative and demonstrated a real passion for his product. Next thing you know, I found myself starting down yet another new path in life. It's amazing how everything just fell into place. That new path ultimately led me to meet Wayde, land my job at ATM, and end up on *Tanked*. When I think of how much some people go through just trying to get on television once, it's mind-blowing to consider that I ended up on a hit show in such a strange, unplanned, indirect way.

In 2006, a big, friendly, personable, jocular guy walked into the dealership, looking to buy a Porsche. He asked a lot of questions about my job selling cars, including whether I'd consider leaving. Wayde told me all about ATM and the amazing custom aquariums they were building for people all over the world. They had so many new orders coming in that they needed extra help in the office. He certainly seemed much easier to deal with compared to a lot of my extremely demanding clients.

When the final papers were ready for the Porsche, I took them over to the ATM facility personally to get his signature and have a look for myself. I loved the family business feel of the place from the moment I walked inside, so I decided to consider taking the job. The luxury car business put me in contact with a lot of fascinating people, but the hours proved crazy, and the income can fluctuate wildly. Moving a single Ferrari can carry you nicely for a month or more, but hit a dry spell and you're screwed. Meanwhile, ATM offered something steady and reliable. I had absolutely no experience with aquariums, but I wasn't afraid to work hard and learn on the job, the same way I got through that first year of school after moving from Poland.

> "I had absolutely no experience with aquariums, but I wasn't afraid to work hard and learn on the job."

So I signed on for yet another new adventure, one that started when I trained to become an estimator for pool panels and related projects. Even the most dedicated *Tanked* fans may not know, but constructing and installing paneling for large swimming pools and commercial aquatic tanks makes up a significant portion of ATM's income every year. It's not as fun or exciting as custom-themed aquariums, so that work doesn't show up on television, but it has been vital to our success.

My first week at work, I had so much to learn and do that I hardly noticed the bare-bones crew running around filming everything. Wayde briefly had mentioned something about a reality TV show to me when he bought the Porsche, but it sounded like a lark. Either way, as the new girl in the office I just kept my head down and focused on the task at hand

without worrying about the cameras. They caught me in one shot while I used the copy machine, which made it into the pilot, but otherwise I didn't get involved. It sounded like a fun idea, but I never thought it would take off. So many people try to do something like that, and it doesn't work out. Nor had I realized yet how big a deal ATM was in the aquarium world.

Two years went by as Brett tried everything under the sun to sell the show. When we heard, after all that time, that Animal Planet was not only interested but ready to start filming, it floored all of us. You don't often get to see a dream come true, especially one that big and difficult to accomplish. It's been a great experience for all of us—but also a little crazy. Kids come in to the ATM office for the tour, and they think we're big celebrities; that's how much they love the show. Knowing that what we do makes them happy thrills me because *Tanked* promotes a lot of positive values for kids.

We try to keep it entertaining and educational without taking ourselves too seriously, then at the end of every episode you see an amazing, unique aquarium. All of the tanks we build are memorable to me because we all have a hand in their creation, whether that means writing a bid, designing the filtration, or just ordering a part. So much goes into building one of these aquariums, including an awful lot that you never see on television. It might be easy to forget, but it's not just the six of us making it happen. More than fifty employees at ATM all contribute to producing these incredible pieces of living art.

People can stare into an aquarium for hours and get lost in it. I do that myself sometimes. Seeing a school of vibrant, colorful fish swimming around always brightens my mood. It's perfectly serene. Some day I'm going to install a jellyfish aquarium in my own home, but I'm waiting until I have enough free time to do all of the care, feeding, and maintenance myself. In the meantime, my big hobby is hitting the poker rooms around town for some Texas Hold 'Em.

I don't play poker a lot—nor should anyone, really—but I love the challenge of it. Focusing on the cards, the odds, and the other competitors takes my mind off everything else in my life in a strangely meditative way. I've only been at it a few years, but I like to think I've become fairly decent. Many of the highest ranking players in the world live right here in Las

Sometimes you need a night out on the town to take your mind off your worries!

Vegas, and we host the biggest cash prize tournaments of the year, so I've had a chance to observe the best card players around, up close and personal.

But my real education started with a bunch of old men around a table at Binion's. First opened in 1951, Binion's Gambling Hall and Hotel founded and hosted the World Series of Poker Tournament from its inception in 1970 until fairly recently. It's one of the few remaining icons from the old Las Vegas Rat Pack era. Where better to learn the game?

Sitting down at one of their legendary tables for the first time, shoehorned in among a bunch of cigar-chomping, rough-talking, gray-haired men, I felt my hands sweating. They all were going to give the cold shoulder to a little blonde newbie like me, I was sure. Instead, they welcomed me and taught me how to play not just the cards but the other players, too. To succeed at poker, you've got to read people's minds and know what they're going to do—a skill I've found useful in all sorts of real life situations. It's one of the best skills that the game has taught me.

I've been trying to get Heather to join me because we hang out all the time and it would be wonderful to have another lady at the table. So far, I haven't been able to convince her to ante up, but I'm not sure how well she'd keep a poker face. Heather really wears her heart on her sleeve, which is one of the traits I love best about her. She also knows how to be a real friend. We've grown so close over the years, which people watching the show recognize and identify with, especially female viewers. Reality TV has almost become the norm these days, and I'm a fan, but so often you see women pitted against one another in some petty dispute or vying for

Heather and I having a blast during the KISS tank unveiling (see page 146)

the same man rather than supporting one another and working together. Heather and I aren't like that; we don't fight or backstab.

In fact, as much as I love feeling like one of the family at ATM, I always stay as far away as possible from their inevitable family arguments. Wayde, Heather, and Irwin all live together in the same house, so they can never really escape from any of it. I don't know how they keep from going crazy sometimes. I mean, I love my family, but I couldn't imagine sharing an office with them, nevermind living with them, too. Still, they make it work while making everyone else feel like family too, which is great, and Wayde still drives the car I sold him!—a Carrera 996.

Every day there's something new happening, and on top of that you've got all the laughing, crying, fighting, and friendship of this big, crazy family. The atmosphere at ATM is organized chaos. Not only are the aquariums custom, so are the people. We have workers with so many different skills under one roof, everything from cutting acrylic to fixing computers. So the show has this wonderful message about what a group of seemingly ordinary people, with extraordinary skills, can accomplish when they set their minds to it and work together.

> "Not only are the aquariums custom, so are the people."

There's a perception that, if you live in Las Vegas, you spend all your time on the Strip, drinking and gambling. Obviously that's not true; we have communities here, and most of us live pretty normal lives. Naturally you have to be careful because the place can suck you in, but I love this town. It's wonderful to know that we're a part of representing Las Vegas to the rest of the world. *Tanked* shows another side of life here, and I feel fortunate to be a part of that.

Agnes Wilczynski
Estimator, ATM

The Vegas Strip at dusk—there's nowhere else like it!

www.AcrylicAquariums.com

n 2013, ATM moved into a new, state-of-the-art production facility with the capacity to fabricate, assemble, and ship more than a thousand custom aquariums each year. The manufacturing area alone spreads out over 33,000 square feet, including 200 square feet devoted to high-pile storage,

The first ATM facility

a 60-square-foot area for making coral inserts, another 60 square feet for plumbing, and 625 square feet for welding and chopping. We've assembled every tool of the trade here as well, including Computer Numerical Control machines that allow a craftsman to control lathes, mills, routers, and grinders by computer. In all, the facility houses about $1 million in equipment, plus a storage bin stocked with $200,000 in supplics at all times. Production never stops just to order parts.

We have four forklifts—including one that can reach 35 feet out to lift the really big tanks—and eight bay doors for eighteen-wheelers to back up right into the shop. At ATM's previous facility, unloading an eighteen-wheeler meant dragging the cargo out with chains. Now they just pull up to the bay doors so the long-reach forklift can get inside. Trucks now unload in minutes when it used to take hours . . . all with a lot less stress on the workers.

Brett horsing around on one of the forklifts in the facility

Hundreds of people visit the facility each week to take the tour and greet us, so there's always a lot of excitement in the air. From spotting Robbie "the Redneck" welding together one of his masterpieces to overhearing the latest office gossip, those who make the pilgrimage will surely catch a glimpse of something unique behind the scenes. At any given time, there are also more than two dozen exotic birds on display, including macaws, blue wings, green wings, red wings, cockatoos, and a toucan. Listen carefully during the next episode of *Tanked,* and you just might hear them in the background.

Pet Detectives

In January 2013, the unthinkable happened. Four exotic birds were stolen from the ATM facility—all of them rescue animals, including Sapphire, a gold macaw with a missing claw. The after-hours burglary was part of a crime spree by a pet-snatching operation that also hit a puppy boutique on the same night, making off with several high-priced breeds, including two white French bulldogs, a gray schnauzer puppy, and a black Yorkshire terrier.

Security cameras captured the robbery in progress, putting police on the trail of two white males in their late teens or early twenties. After coordinating with the authorities, we decided to go public with the story, talking with the press in hopes of generating enough publicity to bring the perpetrators to justice in time to ensure the birds' safe return.

"We love our animals here, so it hurts, like someone taking your kid." Wayde told Las Vegas's ABC News affiliate. "I just can't believe someone actually ran in here in the middle of the night and stole birds."

Officials apprehended the perpetrators within days of the crime and recovered almost all of the birds unharmed. One bird, however, had already been sold by the thieves and remains missing to this day. It was part of a brother-and-sister pair raised together and never separated before. The one we got back is doing okay, but it's sad that they were grabbed and torn apart. "If I had caught somebody doing that I'd probably be in jail," said Wayde.

TOP TANKS

Take a closer look at the most memorable, completely over-the-top builds in ATM history, including a massive home aquarium that never appeared on TV.

NEW YORK CITY PHONE BOOTH TANK

SPECIFICATIONS

Dimensions: 72" H x 44" W x 44" D

Volume: 600 gallons / saltwater

Episode Name: Swimming with the Sharks

Airdate: August 19, 2011

Despite calling Las Vegas home for two decades, we—Wayde, Brett, Heather, and the General—still consider ourselves New Yorkers at heart.

Whether it's pining for a perfect slice of pizza or dreaming of the bright lights on Broadway, we understand exactly how it feels to leave the Big Apple behind while still longing for another bite.

So when Bill and Kathy, fellow NYC expats living in Vegas, contacted us about a special New York–themed aquarium for their home office, the ideas started flowing immediately: a taxi cab, a subway car, the Statue of Liberty.

"Once he started talking about New York, my heart began racing," Brett admitted. "I started getting really excited, and so what do you expect me to do?"

Turns out, Wayde expected him to come up with a workable concept all on his own. Brett started with an exploratory trip to the junkyard, where he

tracked down a little piece of his old stomping grounds and dragged it back to the office.

"My vision for Kathy and Bill's aquarium is to re-create a New York City street scene," he explained. "This phone booth, the centerpiece, will be turned into an aquarium by removing the interior and most of the panels. Then we will build an acrylic tank for the phone booth shell to slide over. All the life support [pumps, filters, etc.] will be on the other side of the wall, behind the tank, which will reduce noise and save space, and we'll have theming items inside the tank plus New York props on the outside like a streetlamp, a real fire hydrant, and a mural of the Manhattan skyline."

Seeing a $100 junkyard phone booth with a broken door instead of his brother-in-law's grand vision, Wayde was less than impressed. He doubted the clients would sign off on Brett's idea as a real New York aquarium since phone booths once stood on nearly every corner in every city all across America. But Brett knew just how to sell the idea.

"Remember the old days?" he asked Bill and Kathy, "when there were no cell phones, no pagers, no beepers . . ."

"I actually spent a lot of time in phone booths," Bill replied. "It does bring back a lot of memories of trying to do business in one of those. I always especially loved finding one with a door on it—that was a big thing, like having your own private office in the city."

To fill the tank and make sure the fish stay visible, Wayde recommended schools of fifteen to twenty in diverse colors and varieties, to represent the various different neighborhoods in New York, like Little Italy, Chinatown, and Greenwich Village. At Exotic Reef Imports, we found schooling fish, including yellowtail damsels, with a blue body to represent the NYPD, red

squirrels to represent the FDNY fire trucks, yellow tangs sustainably collected in Hawaii to represent taxi cabs, and multicolored domino damsels to represent everyone else.

"First thing we're gonna do with the phone is remove the insides so they don't corrode underwater and damage the fish," Brett said, "and then we're gonna turn the entire headset into a bubbler. That's gonna look really cool."

But the phone booth aquarium proved difficult to install. A minor measuring error led to cutting a hole in the acrylic that didn't line up with the water and filtration system.

"The plumbing goes through the tank at holes called bulkheads," Brett explained. "The acrylic of the tank is so thick that we have to cut two holes, one from the outside and one from the inside. Turns out, we cut the inside hole in the wrong spot, so now it won't seal, which means the tank won't hold water—and that ain't good!"

> "Turns out, we cut the inside hole in the wrong spot, so now it won't seal, which means the tank won't hold water—and that ain't good!"

Luckily, we had an even bigger saw on hand, so we cut one of the holes large enough to make everything match up. As usual, everything came together perfectly just before the big unveiling. But with two hard-nosed New Yorkers waiting to evaluate their work, we took nothing for granted . . . until we saw the huge smiles on Bill and Kathy's faces.

"We actually feel like we're on a street corner back in New York," Bill said, offering the greatest compliment that Brett could imagine for this aquarium. "That really hits home and touches us both personally. I couldn't have pictured anything better than this. You guys really outdid yourselves!"

What You Didn't See on TV

From the beginning, we anticipated getting this tank into the house through a set of sliding glass doors in the back, but when we got there it actually cleared the front door by a quarter inch. For once we had an easier time installing a tank than we expected.

Featured Fish
Yellowtail Damsel
Seen in: New York City Phone Booth Tank

Selected to represent the New York Police Department, yellowtail damsels (*Chrysiptera parasema*) do the boys in blue proud with their bright coloring, offset by their namesake yellow tails. They're also an extremely hardy aquarium fish: not overly aggressive compared to similar breeds and capable of living happily in a tank of only 30 gallons. Best kept in a small group of odd numbered fish that can swim together in a school, they love places to hide out in a tank and must be kept apart from certain aggressive species. Native to the reefs of the Indo-Pacific, these omnivores reach a maximum size of just 3 inches when raised in an aquarium and need a diet of zooplankton and algae supplemented with meaty treats like vitamin-enriched shrimp. Slow, steady eaters, they thrive best when provided with several smaller meals per day.

THE MOB EXPERIENCE TANK

SPECIFICATIONS

Dimensions: 48" H x 96"x 96" W (L shape) x 36" D

Volume: 1,160 gallons / saltwater

Episode Name: Swimming with the Sharks

Airdate: August 19, 2011

Thanks to countless movies and television shows, Americans from all walks of life have an abiding fascination for organized crime, particularly the larger-than-life Mob bosses who have captured the popular imagination by eliciting a thrilling mix of fear, awe, and even envy from the vast majority of us who never (or seldom) break the law. From *The Godfather* to *The*

Taking a look at the props for the tank

Sopranos, the Mafia of old and their modern-day descendants populate so many enduring classic films that their world has evolved into a genre all its own, right alongside westerns, science fiction, and vampire tales.

Growing up in New York, Wayde and Brett both knew a few guys in their respective neighborhoods who might have understood a thing or two about the Mob—and not from sitting in a Cineplex. When the opportunity came along to add a one-of-a-kind ATM custom aquarium to The Mob Experience, an all-new attraction at the Tropicana Hotel on the strip, well, they knew it was an offer that they couldn't refuse.

Through a mix of character actors, hologram celebrities, and authentic artifacts, the 27,000-square-foot immersive, interactive experience chronicles the history of the original gangsters who built Las Vegas from the sand up. "We have a collection of over one thousand artifacts—probably the largest Mob-themed collection in the world," Lou Ventre, one of the exhibit's partners, told us when we checked it out. "We've even got 'Bugsy' Siegel's 1933 Packard limo and 'Lucky' Luciano's 1927 Studebaker."

Once Lou explained that the aquarium would be the first thing people see as they approach the attraction, we all knew it had to be special . . . or we might end up sleeping with the fishes.

"Man, I got a great idea," Brett blurted. "Why don't we put flat-screen TVs inside the tank?"

Wayde could hardly believe his ears and didn't know how they'd ever pull it off, but playing scenes from classic Mob movies inside a gangster-themed

> We all knew it had to be special . . . or we might end up sleeping with the fishes.

aquarium would definitely make an amazing first impression. Shaped like a giant L that wraps around the corner of the lobby, we designed and built a tank that features two flat-screen monitors sealed in acrylic casing to keep them dry. Installing the casing required flipping the entire

tank upside down—always difficult—and even more so with an oddly shaped aquarium. During the flip the acrylic creaked quite a bit, but thankfully we didn't have any cracks or crashes.

When it came time to fill the tank, we sought out tough looking breeds to fit the theme, like naso tangs, a Brazilian queen angel, a blue-ring angel, feather dusters, regal angels, an Achilles tang, parrot fish, and blue dark triggers.

To get the tank in place, we had to demolish the section of the wall where it would sit, then roll in its steel frame and slide the tank on top. Then we installed the TV screens and theming items, like a stick of dynamite, tommy guns, and a pair of cement shoes taken directly off Brett's feet.

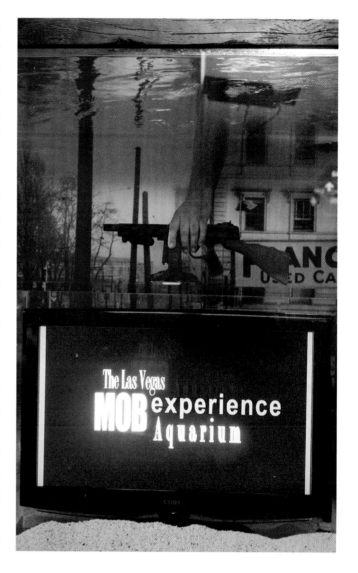

When we hooked up the water input and started filling the tank, however, we had only a hot water line to work with, which poured out at a scorching 92 degrees. Way too hot to add the fish, which were still swimming around in the small plastic shipping containers they'd arrived in.

"If they go in at that temperature, they'll die!" Wayde despaired. "But we can't leave them in their containers too long or they'll deplete all of the oxygen."

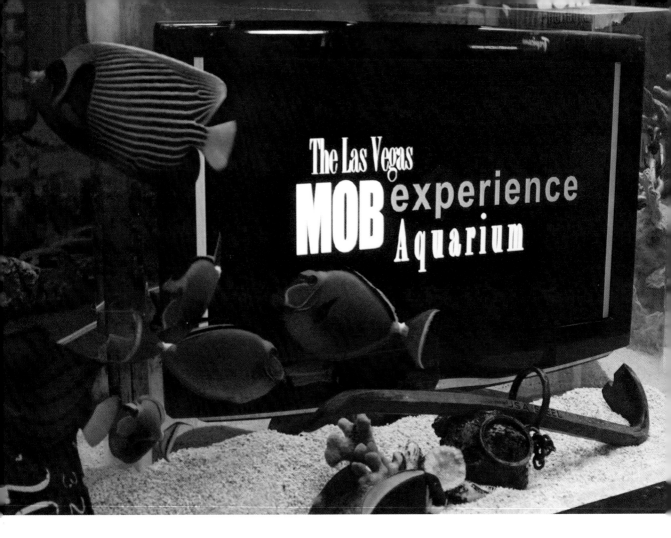

Thinking fast, Wayde realized that the massive hotel could make enough ice and fast enough to bring the tank's temperature down to something comfortable for all of the marine life they had waiting on deck.

"Only after we got the temperature, pH, salinity, and everything else perfect would we ever add our fish to their new home," Wayde explained. "Wouldn't want any of them to end up getting whacked!"

What You Didn't See on TV

The tank had working TVs built into it, so we did a funny commercial featuring the entire ATM team dressed up as mobsters. The video played when we first unveiled the tank for our clients, but it never made it onto the show.

Featured Fish
Feather Duster
Seen in: The Mob Experience

Despite their highly exotic appearance, feather dusters (*Sabellastarte spectabilis*) are actually easy to deal with in an aquarium. They have a hearty life force and a peaceful demeanor. Capable of growing up to 7 inches long in captivity, they're best known for the fan-shaped tan- or orange-colored crown that they use to filter the water for tiny organisms pushed toward their mouths and eaten. Natural omnivores native to Hawaii and the Indo-Pacific, they're usually found toward the bottom of a reef aquarium, where they like to patrol for plankton. When facing undue aggression from another species or suffering any type of severe stress, they might pull their sifters into their bodies or even drop them entirely. The sifters grow back anew when the danger has passed.

DALLAS MEGACHURCH TANK

SPECIFICATIONS

Dimensions: 17' H x 70' W x 10' D

Volume: 70,000 gallons / saltwater

Episode name: Be Cool

Airdate: September 2, 2011

Dubbed the "Fishtine Chapel," this aquarium serves as a glorious entryway for the Inspiring Body of Christ Church in Dallas, Texas, part of a 176,000-square-foot worship facility that serves as the hub of IBOC's 36-acre campus, where more than seven thousand people attend services each week.

One of the largest and most complex builds in ATM history, the aquarium takes its inspiration from the church's official motto, words spoken by Jesus to his disciples when he asked them to quit their jobs as fishermen, renounce material wealth and worldly possessions, and join him instead: "Follow me, and I will make you fishers of men."

At a cost of more than $4.7 million, the massive tank forms just one part of the newly erected $40 million IBOC church, which took fifty laborers two years to finish and literally had to be constructed around the stunning aquarium that serves as its arched portal. More than six hundred fish call it home, and the church even employs a full-time marine biologist to keep all those creatures healthy and happy in a clean, properly maintained environment. Species in the tank include blue tangs, French grunts, nurse sharks, and stingrays.

IBOC's Pastor Rush sees it all as evidence of God's plan for all of His creations to live together in peace and harmony. "Fish come in so many different species, but they all live in the same waters," he says. "All of us people come from so many different places, but we all live in the same world! That's what I really hope everyone will get from this aquarium."

As the awe-inspiring tank's official dedication ceremony drew near, however, Pastor Rush found himself compelled to request one last addition to the tank: not another fish but a five-foot cross made of artificial coral. No problem there, but it needed to be built and installed in just *five days*. Not exactly a miracle—but a heck of a lot of work in a very short time. To make sure all ran smoothly, Brett and Wayde agreed to oversee the cross's design, construction, and installation personally.

First, we built a wooden frame and covered it with epoxy to waterproof the wood and give it a slightly weathered look. Once that dried, we added a layer of paint before covering the cross in artificial coral modeled on living coral. Creating and arranging coral in a way that looks natural takes real

artistry, and ATM employs some of the best in the world at doing it right, even under the tightest of deadlines. By the time the *Tanked* team arrived in Dallas with the finished product, we barely had a minute to spare, and every seat in the house was taken for the big unveiling.

"When I went to that church on a Sunday morning and it filled up with three thousand people who walked under those arches through those tunnels I felt goosebumps," Wayde recalls. "To watch them all look into that tank in amazement and wonder was such an achievement that it still gives me chills. Knowing something I built will be there far longer than I'm alive, that's just thrilling and humbling."

Donning his wetsuit and preparing to enter this unorthodox "holy water," however, Wayde still had to put up with one of his brother-in-law's wisecracks: "You look like a seal," Brett quipped. "Just not a Navy Seal." Jokes aside, Wayde had to contend with a big problem: The cross kept rising to the surface of the tank as he tried to install it. Thousands of people were packing the pews, the cameras were rolling, and maybe even God was watching. It would have been extremely embarrassing to have a floating cross ruin the pastor's big moment.

> Keeping calm—and helped perhaps by a bit of divine intervention—Wayde realized that his troubles were coming from a small pocket of air trapped inside the coral cross.

Keeping calm—and helped perhaps by a bit of divine intervention—Wayde realized that his troubles were coming from a small pocket of air trapped inside the coral cross. So he tipped it over, let the air escape, and finished the installation before anyone (aside from the Almighty) was any the wiser.

What You Didn't See on TV

In addition to the so-called "Fishtine Chapel," we also built two other tanks at that same location: a 2,500-gallon cylinder and a 200-gallon tank in the office. Altogether, it's definitely one of the most impressive custom jobs we've ever built.

WAYDE'S OCTOPUS TANK

To surprise Wayde on his birthday, Heather decided to have a special aquarium installed in his office while he wasn't looking—no easy task considering the long hours Wayde spends at his desk and the keen eye with which he follows everything and anything that goes on in the ATM production facility. To get this one past him, she had to recruit a few accomplices from the *Tanked* team while engaging in just a little bit of deception.

> Heather had to recruit a few accomplices from the *Tanked* team while engaging in just a little bit of deception.

The theme for this particularly personal tank harkened back to their honeymoon in Hawaii when Wayde fulfilled a lifelong dream by swimming with an octopus. Knowing that he'd been obsessing over the idea of an octopus tank ever since, Heather wanted to make that happen for him. She also felt like the octopus would be a perfect symbol for Wayde's personality: "He's always trying to juggle eight things at once."

The first person Heather approached for help was naturally Robbie the Redneck. It's the thought that counts of course, but he had to do most of the work. He was willing to put in the time to make a nice surprise for Wayde, but didn't think the theme that Heather had in mind was particularly wise. "Octopuses are conniving little creatures that will try to escape," he explained. "I have to make this thing like a safe or you'll come in and find its tentacles wrapped around Wayde's computer monitor."

Heather helping to fill the aquarium between Wayde's office and Brett's

That didn't deter Heather in the least. "That's all on you. Just pretend that I'm any other ATM customer, and give me what I want."

In the end, they struck a deal. Redneck built a beautiful octopus tank, but Heather helped. She recruited Agnes as her assistant, and the two women took a crash course in how to polish acrylic in order to add a bit of their own elbow grease to the effort. Meanwhile, Heather also enlisted brother Brett to acquire the required octopus (by stealth) during his next trip to Exotic Reef Imports in Los Angeles and bring it back without Wayde's knowledge. He returned, undetected, with a mimic octopus, so-called because they can match the movements and appearance of at least fifteen different ocean species, including sea snakes, lionfish, and giant crabs. They also grow to be only two feet long when kept in a tank, which made it an ideal choice for an office tank.

Of course, the surprise almost got ruined when Wayde grew suspicious and started snooping around, but Heather knew her man well enough to

concoct a brilliant plan. She bought him ice cream as a distraction, throwing him off the track by calling that his birthday surprise, a misdirection that worked like a charm. When it came time for the dramatic unveiling, Wayde never saw it coming. But first, Heather had to spend a little quality bonding time with the newest addition to the ATM staff.

"I've always found octopuses to be kind of creepy and slimy," she admitted, "but looking at this guy, he's so cute I think I might be having a change of heart."

For Wayde, it was another case of love at first sight: "I really can't believe what they did for me," he said, clearly touched by the gesture. "I work really hard, long hours. So to have this badass tank right in my office, I couldn't ask for anything more."

A mimic octopus

SKATEBOARD RAMP TANK

SPECIFICATIONS

Dimensions: 48" H x 84" W x 48" D

Volume: 840 gallons / saltwater

Episode Name: Tricks of the Trade

Airdate: September 16, 2011

As the world's premier apparel licensing company, The La Jolla Group works with the most recognized names in the surf, skate, and action sports industries to help market those brands to the world. Naturally they wanted a custom aquarium as extreme as their company and their clientele. Ryan Divel, a vice president at La Jolla, gave us a tour of their office, pointing out that they already had one tank in their headquarters, but they wanted another that would take it to the next level.

"We want something bigger, badder, crazier," he explained. "I want a ramp aquarium hybrid conjoined thing together."

Somehow able to make sense of this request, Brett confirmed that ATM's newest client desired an aquarium that would double as a working ramp to accommodate the many employees in the office who zipped from one end of the sizable operation to the other on skateboards, scooters, and even more exotic contraptions. It would be one of the most difficult builds we'd ever attempted but one of the coolest, too—if we could pull it off.

"We want something bigger, badder, crazier."

The biggest challenge was achieving the precise curvature of the working ramp, which required bending the acrylic perfectly so it would give a good ride while supporting the weight of the rider with plenty of strength to spare. We started with an 8-foot-long, 4-foot-high, 800-gallon rectangular tank, then formed a J-shaped radium on the front of it to create a seamless

transition from the base of the ramp to the acrylic. Beneath the sturdy steel stand, we left room to accommodate all of the plumbing and life-support systems necessary to keep the water clean and healthy.

To test the strength of the acrylic, Wayde took it for a ride himself, despite his extremely limited skateboarding experience in the past. Unfortunately, he couldn't get moving fast enough to make it up the ramp. "I haven't pushed this hard since my last kidney stone!" he joked while waiting for a local pro skater to come over and give the acrylic a true test.

The skate pro's first run up the ramp left noticeable scratches on the surface, so we junked that prototype and started all over again, this time putting the acrylic in the oven at a higher temperature for a shorter period of time, so it would come out much harder and resistant to abrasion.

Inside the tank, we developed a surf/skate theme to highlight the company's lifestyle roots and feature some of their top brands. Playful touches like a surfboard with a huge bite taken out and a "No Swimming: Sharks" sign reinforced the aquarium's feeling of playful menace. Even the fish that filled it were gnarly, like a vibrant orange saddle wrasse from Hawaii, a gray smooth-hound shark, rusty angels, porcupine puffers, a lionfish with a debilitating sting, and a huge koran fish destined to rule the tank. It became an instant conversation piece from the moment it was installed.

The ramp aquarium made an undeniably impressive addition to La Jolla's official office skate zone—especially once the staff discovered that they could ride as hard and fast as any other ramp despite it being fully stocked with fish.

"Oh my gosh!" Ryan yelled out after his first glimpse. "This thing is mental. I'm tripping right now!"

What You Didn't See on TV

Wayde grew up skateboarding, and he was zipping through the warehouse on one of the boards so well that it surprised the whole production staff. When the episode aired, it showed only the part when he fell down—which of course was funny!

Featured Fish
Porcupine Puffer
Seen in: Skateboard Ramp Tank

Named for the spiny, quill-like appendages that cover most of their bodies and their ability, when threatened, to inflate themselves to twice their normal size, Porcupine puffers (*Diodon holocanthus*) have no pelvic fins whatsoever, so they have to use their well-developed pectoral fins to move in the water. Capable of growing up to 1 foot in length, they require aquariums of at least 180 gallons, preferably with a high-quality protein skimmer to keep tank pollution down. Native to the Caribbean, this moderately aggressive omnivore will occasionally take a nip at other fish kept alongside it, leaving a distinctly circular hole behind. Anyone taking a bite back in return, however, should be warned that parts of this fish's flesh can be poisonous if ingested.

VINTAGE PINBALL MACHINE TANK

SPECIFICATIONS

Dimensions: one 30" H x 30" W x 18" D and two
18" H x 48" W x 12" D

Volume: one 70 gallon, two 56 gallon / freshwater

Episode name: Old School versus New School

Airdate: April 21, 2012

When the call came in to create a special new tank for a conservation police officer who loves nothing more than old-school pinball machines and state-of-the-art aquariums we started with an intense research and development session. Which meant paying Jed a home visit so we could spend a few blissful hours in his basement full of vintage arcade games without having to pump the machines full of quarters.

Jed already had a beautiful and lovingly maintained 20-foot aquarium upstairs, so the new addition had to fit the basement's decor while adding a little wow factor to one of the best "man caves" ever seen on the show. When Brett suggested transforming a working, vintage pinball machine into an eye-popping themed aquarium, we all knew that's exactly what had to be done. The only question: How?

"You know, I really think that's a cool idea," said Wayde, "but I really don't know how we're going to do this."

As every dedicated *Tanked* fan knows, however, once we agree to make an aquarium dream into a reality, we can't stop and won't until the job gets done. Not that such pledges of honor kept Wayde from getting more than a little ticked off at Brett for opening his big mouth—as usual.

"A functional pinball machine has components, a switchboard, wires all over the place," Wayde reminded his perpetually overenthusiastic partner. "What's next, we build a rocket ship aquarium that really works?"

"That sounds like a great idea," Brett replied. "I better go call NASA."

Back at the ATM production facility in Las Vegas, the *Tanked* team settled into a serious brainstorming effort. But we were really just spinning our wheels until the General came up with the brilliant idea of taking a field trip to the nearby Pinball Hall of Fame and Museum. Created by the Las Vegas Pinball Collectors Club, the 10,000-square-foot facility features classic pinball machines, wall-to-wall, many dating back to the 1950s, all restored to like-new condition.

"I played some of these machines before you boys were even born," the General reminisced.

Brett and Wayde, meanwhile, began searching for a suitable framework to transform into the tank of Jed's dreams. When we came across a pirate-themed pinball machine featuring images of Poseidon, stingrays, schools of fish, and a shark, we knew we had found our starting place. Just one problem. Tim Arnold, the man behind the museum, wouldn't sell it—at any price.

> "These machines are my friends," he told us. "You don't sell your friends."

"These machines are my friends," he told us. "You don't sell your friends."

Fortunately, some quick research revealed that exactly 3,006 such machines had been built in 1977, and Tim knew somebody local who had an identical machine and could be convinced to part with it at the right price and for such a worthy cause. Still, that was just the beginning of the challenges facing us, particularly Robbie the Redneck, who was none too happy with this particular assignment.

"You weren't thinking," he complained to Brett when faced with the technical challenges involved and the typically near-impossible deadline. "You were just selling, like usual!"

Still, Redneck and everyone else at ATM went full-tilt to make it happen. The design called for two freshwater tanks to run along the sides of the pinball machine, each supported by its own steel stand. Plus a third tank

situated in front of the back glass of the machine so that players can still admire their high scores while looking directly through a working aquarium. Tim from the Pinball Hall of Fame, intrigued by the project, even showed up to help with the retrofitting of the scoreboard, which involved extending all of the wiring at least three feet using spare parts salvaged from similar machines made by the same manufacturer in the same year.

"It's like a pinball machine organ donation," Wayde joked.

Another challenge involved reconciling a serious difference between aquariums, which need to be level, and pinball machines, which need to slope down to the player so the ball remains in motion at all times. After figuring out a workable way to adjust the tanks' stands accordingly, disaster struck when Brett accidentally broke the glass in front of the scoreboard while trying to move it into place.

At that point, Jed had already made arrangements to fly friends in to witness his grand basement unveiling, which meant there was no time to lose. So we started the install without the broken glass panel, hoping to have everything ready for a replacement to arrive at the very last minute. After unraveling and reassembling a rat's nest of wires and plugs, all of which had to connect correctly for all of the machine's lights and bells to work, we hired an artist to paint a custom mural around the tank to tie all of our work together.

When the replacement glass finally arrived, there was just enough time to fill the machine's three separate tanks with live plants, driftwood, albino angel fish, rainbow fish, and fluorescent zebra fish before the big moment. All in all, it was an incredible amount of work, but it was all worth it to see Jed's smile and hear him proclaim that ATM's latest piece of living art "far and away exceeded" all of his expectations.

What You Didn't See on TV

That machine was really hard to take apart because of all the wiring. We worked through the night to get all the soldering done on schedule. But spending time with such a cool vintage machine brought us back to good times growing up.

MINUS 5 ICE BAR TANK

SPECIFICATIONS

Dimensions: 30" H x 48" W x 18" D

Volume: 112 gallons / saltwater

Episode Name: Polar Opposites

Airdate: May 19, 2012

Wayde loved Minus 5 Ice Bar from the moment he walked inside, but the concept left Brett feeling a little . . . well, cold. "Maybe I'd like it more if I had as much insulation as you," he kidded his brother-in-law.

Housed in the Monte Carlo Resort and Casino on the Las Vegas Strip, the fully functional high-end cocktail lounge is kept at a perpetually frosty 23 degrees Fahrenheit (-5 Celsius). No easy feat when temperatures outside occasionally reach 120 degrees!

Once inside Minus 5, however, you'd never suspect that you were standing in the middle of the desert, especially once you don the special winter parkas, hats, and gloves given to all customers to keep them warm while enjoying a totally unique nightlife experience, where everything including the bar, tables, and chairs has been carved out of solid ice using chainsaws, blowtorches, and chisels. It took special artisans weeks to build and needed only one addition to put it over the top: an aquarium tank fully encrusted in ice!

"First we need to make sure it's a fish tank and not an ice cube," Brett realized. "Also, heat and ice don't mix, so we have to be very careful about how we keep the water warm because any little bit of heat could cause melting inside the bar and ruin everything, literally shutting this place down for weeks. Something as simple as setting down a soldering iron could melt a hole right into the ice."

Still, despite those reservations and a lingering case of the shivers, Brett came up with the vision for this truly one-of-a-kind tank: translucent jellyfish, which can live in cooler water than most other marine life, with an ethereal appearance that's a perfect match for the Ice Bar decor. Now all we needed to do was import the jellies from the Philippines and figure out how to get the tank to a steady 60 degrees.

To test the aquarium before installing it, Wayde had Heather rent a walk-in freezer set to the same temperature as the bar. The original plan called for using a submergible heater calibrated to keep the water warm enough for jellyfish without radiating any heat out through the tank's 1¼-inch acrylic walls.

Translucent jellyfish

But after less than an hour in the freezer, the aquarium turned to ice. So we switched to a system using an in-line heater instead that constantly heats the tank from underneath. It cost ten times as much, but that's what had to be done. The tank's filtration system also had to be specially designed because jellyfish are so fragile and require a gentle current to keep them in the center of the tank, away from harm.

When the aquarium was finally ready to install inside Minus 5, we filled it slowly with warm water to prevent shocking or cracking the acrylic

with a rapid temperature change. But the motor for the heater pushed too hard and popped a circuit, putting the entire install in peril and plunging the bar into darkness. Everything was about to start melting!

Luckily an electrician from the casino arrived to put the aquarium pump and heater on their own circuit before restoring power. Next the ice carvers got to work integrating the aquarium into the bar. Before long, the jellyfish were swimming around happily in their new home.

"It's just amazing," Noel Bowman, president of the Minus 5 Ice Bar, told Brett and Wayde upon witnessing their handiwork for the first time. "I just can't wait until everyone can see this!"

The finished tank in place

Agnes agrees and still calls it her all-time favorite ATM tank.

"Minus 5 Ice Bar was our coolest aquarium—literally!" She says. "Everything is made of ice . . . the walls, the seats, the lights, even the glasses you drink from. At minus 5 degrees Celsius, even the faux fur coats Heather and I had on didn't keep us warm . . . we were freezing! I thought my nose was going to fall off, and I still have no idea how Wayde and Brett withstood that chill for hours as they installed the jellyfish tank in the bar."

What You Didn't See on TV

Sculpting the ice at this bar was a lot of fun. Wayde tried his hand at it a few times as a kid, so working with professionals in that field was exciting and brought out his creativity.

KISS TRIBUTE TANK

SPECIFICATIONS

Dimensions: 48" H x 96" W x 30" D

Volume: 570 gallons / saltwater

Episode Name: Where the Wild Things Are

Airdate: June 9, 2012

One of the most successful recording and touring acts of the 1970s, KISS has earned twenty-eight gold albums to date, more than any other American rock band. Best known for monster hits like "Rock and Roll All Night," "Detroit Rock City," and "Love Gun," the band embodies the title of rock royalty as few others do.

Forever associated with the arena rock era they helped herald with cartoonish personas, elaborate makeup, massive riffs, chant-along lyrics, and intense stage spectacles featuring circus freaks, fake blood, hovering drum kits, and intense pyrotechnic displays, the band decided to work with ATM when they personally wanted to approve an aquarium for a KISS-themed mini-golf course in Las Vegas. When Agnes first brought in the contract, she could hardly contain her excitement.

Brett takes a break for some air guitar while filling the tank.

"KISS was on the stereo when I had my first kiss," she recalled. "The Camaros, the big hair . . . those were the days."

"You're telling me? I dressed up as KISS once for Halloween!" Brett replied.

We took a field trip to the mini-golf course to check it out. One of more than thirty locations nationwide, these golf courses are typically built around "scary but cool" cartoon monster themes, but the Las Vegas location is based on KISS instead. They'd already amassed an impressive collection of memorabilia related to the band, and they wanted to top it off with an amazing ATM aquarium.

After rocking out and some serious brainstorming, Wayde and Brett hit on the idea of a big tank encased by huge speakers with the instantly recognizable KISS logo re-created inside. Only one catch: KISS themselves were going to attend the grand opening, including the aquarium unveiling. If any one of them didn't think the tank was totally perfect down to

the smallest detail, they might have made us toss it out and start over again from scratch. That's a lot of pressure, but as a fellow perfectionist Wayde could understand the sentiment . . . even when the band began making changes to the plans before giving their approval.

"The guys from KISS want to give the tank a bow-front face," Brett explained. "It's actually a great idea. The whole thing will look like center stage at a rock show, and we'll surround the tank with amplifiers and install lights under the acrylic KISS logo."

The biggest illumination challenge involved making sure everything inside the tank popped amid the relative darkness of the indoor miniature golf course.

"LED lights are the way to go for this job," Brett decided. "They're energy efficient and compact, so we can get a lot of light to shine beneath the letters in the KISS logo."

Agnes frequently checked on the tank's progress during construction, heartily approving the theme and execution. She even helped pick out the fish to fill it, one breed to represent each of the four band members:

Band Member	Persona	Fish
Gene Simmons	The Demon	lionfish
Paul Stanley	Starchild	clown grouper
Peter Criss	Catman	striped heniochus
Ace Frehley	Spaceman	personifier fish

"When it came time to do the reveal for the KISS tank, I was so excited I didn't know what to do with myself," Agnes admitted, increasingly star struck. "Then I was just staring at the door when the band walked in!"

Best of all, each member of the band identified strongly with the fish selected in his honor, and they unanimously declared the ATM tank to

Agnes in shock after Gene Simmons kissed her hand

> They unanimously declared the ATM tank to be totally KISS-worthy.

be totally KISS-worthy. Agnes even got a kiss on the hand from Simmons, one of her all-time heartthrob crushes. She promptly vowed never to wash it again!

What You Didn't See on TV

Those guys are so incredibly famous. When they showed up, tons of people wanted to meet them, so we had to wait. When we finally got a chance to hang out, however, they were all very down to earth, and they genuinely loved our aquarium!

Featured Fish
Lionfish
Seen in: KISS Tank

When the ATM team got offered the unbelievable opportunity to create a custom aquarium in honor of one of their favorite rock bands of all time, KISS, they decided to personalize it by selecting a specific breed to represent each of the four members' on-stage personas, starting with lead singer Gene Simmons as a visually stunning lionfish (*Pterois volitans*). A semi-aggressive variety that's native to the Caribbean, Indonesia, and Africa, this species makes an incredible first impression with fan-like pectoral fins, bold striping, and extreme spines that protrude from its dorsal fins.

Natural carnivores, they grow quickly in captivity, to 15 inches or even larger, and require a tank of no less than 120 gallons, ideally with several places to hide among rocks and coral during their transition into a new home. If they refuse food at first, try tempting them with live saltwater feeder shrimp, a particular delicacy they typically find irresistible.

TRACY MORGAN SHARK TANK

SPECIFICATIONS

Dimensions: 4' H x 20' W x 5' D

Volume: 3,000 gallons / saltwater

Episode Name: We're Gonna Need a Bigger Tank

Airdate: August 11, 2012

Every morning on arriving at ATM headquarters, Brett starts his work routine exactly the same way: checking his Twitter account and watching talk shows in his office with the door closed. It drives Wayde crazy, naturally, but one fine day even Wayde had to admit that Brett's little ritual ended up paying off big time.

It all started when Tracy Morgan—star of *30 Rock*, *Saturday Night Live* alum, and author of the bestselling memoir *I Am the New Black*—was appearing as a guest on *The View,* chatting away with the ladies of daytime

A replica of Wayde's leg for the shark tank

A replica of Brett's arm

TV about his life and career. Usually Brett just keeps *The View* on for background noise while going through his e-mails and getting organized for the day ahead, but on this occasion his ears pricked up the second he heard Whoopi Goldberg ask her special guest about his fish tank.

"I heard you have all kinds of strange things in your aquarium, like piranhas, and that your kids have to know not to put their hands in there," she said. "I heard that you've got jellyfish and stuff that can eat you."

"I love all exotic animals," Tracy replied. "Most people don't even know these creatures exist on the Earth with us."

Brett had already looked up from his e-mail to give the show his undivided attention, but what he heard next nearly made him fall straight out of his seat.

"I want to get a shark tank in my house," Tracy said straight into the camera. "There's a program on TV called *Tanked* on Animal Planet, and I'm asking those guys please to come to my house and build me a nice big shark tank."

Brett could hardly believe his ears. Not only did one of the funniest actors on television want a custom tank, he *asked* for it on national television! Millions of viewers had seen and heard it all happen live on TV, but as far as Brett knew he was the only one at the office who had any idea. What a wonderful feeling!—to know that one of the biggest events in ATM history had just happened and he would get to tell everyone the good news.

> Not only did one of the funniest actors on television want a custom tank, he *asked* for it on national television!

"Wait, can we back this up here a second?" Wayde asked before the importance of the moment had a chance to sink in. "I'm conducting my third business meeting of the day, and you're watching *The View*?"

Brett explained that this would mean a ton of free publicity not to mention a chance to make an amazing aquarium and show it to the world. Tracy Morgan may be famous for his unpredictable behavior and outlandish comedy, but he's also a serious aquarist who has been keeping large and exotic tanks for many years.

"Dude, it's so surreal I can't believe it," Wayde said when the moment finally sank in. Then he told Brett to get Morgan on the phone as soon as possible.

It took a few calls, but within hours of hearing his request Brett was talking with Tracy himself. Sure enough, he couldn't have been more serious about wanting ATM to build him the ultimate home shark tank for his house in New Jersey. He had a lot of ideas about where he wanted the aquarium, which would run the entire length of one wall in his basement, and he knew he wanted sharks. But beyond that, he put his full faith in the *Tanked* team to create a theme and design far beyond anything even his own wild imagination could dream up.

"Whatever you guys put down there I'm gonna love," he told Brett after they agreed to meet for a full consultation. "If I ever get enough money, I want you to build my next house around my fish tank. I want an orca tank!"

When they first flew out to visit Tracy and take measurements, Wayde worried that Brett would be too busy trying to hang out with a celebrity to focus on work. Worse still, maybe he'd make himself a nuisance. But when they arrived at his house, Tracy was more excited about the project than both of them put together. In fact, he greeted them at his front door literally jumping up and down yelling: "ATM is here! ATM is here! Oh my god!"

Morgan introduced Brett and Wayde to his son Tracy Junior and his fiancée, Megan. They took a tour of the eight fish tanks he already had in the house, including one that Megan keeps as her own private aquarium with seventeen moon jellyfish, known for their translucent bodies and ethereal beauty. Tracy's biggest tank held a couple of legendary predators: a green moray eel and a lively sand shark.

"There's only one way in and one way out of my man cave," the star explained as he finished the tour with a visit to the spot where the new shark tank would reside . . . which was actually a problem because the tight angle of the stairs made it extremely difficult to get such a huge tank down to the basement.

After a lot of figuring, we determined that the only way to make it work was with fiberglass-reinforced plastic that could be cut into pieces small enough to fit down stairs, then reassembled in the basement.

"Building a tank like this is a huge risk," Wayde admitted. "Instead of assembling it in the shop we have to put it together like a puzzle on the job site. If our acrylic window doesn't hold the water weight, Tracy's going to have a nice new pool in his basement."

With such a high profile client and the cameras rolling, that would be a huge disaster on several levels, so Wayde put Robbie "the Redneck" and the rest of his top fabricators on the case while another team went to work coming up with the overall design. After some creative riffing and much deliberation, Tracy signed off on a *Jaws* theme that included severed body parts strewn about on the "bottom of the sea" as if ripped off by a shark's razor-sharp teeth.

Viewable through three acrylic windows into the fiberglass tank, the massive shark aquarium transformed the formerly sedate room into an unforgettable interactive experience. We even made the outside of the tank look like the doomed ship from the movie, a decorative façade that also camouflaged the seams in the fiberglass. It was truly unlike anything we had ever built before, especially for a private home. To show just how personal the project had become, we even had a leg (Wayde) and an arm (Brett) cast in plaster to make the models for the severed limbs.

Then we headed to Exotic Reef Imports to select the amazing marine life to do justice to our latest work of "living art." We started with bat rays and stingrays, which come from the same family of predators as sharks, and ordered a blacktip shark and a whitetip shark flown 8,000 miles from Bali to the job site. Both sharks can grow to 6 feet or longer in a tank over the course of two years, with more than a hundred razor-sharp teeth in multiple rows.

Not many smaller fish could survive in a tank with such serious predators, so we chose convict tangs specifically because they'd be able to get in there and hold their own with the sharks and rays. The ultimate schooling fish, those tangs swim in schools of thousands in the open oceans off Fiji.

When the time came for the incredibly complex installation, we traveled back to New Jersey with high hopes of winning Tracy's everlasting acclaim and affection . . . only to find that the special fiberglass panels that we had designed wouldn't fit inside the house. We had to tear the front door's molding out—which wasn't exactly the kind of first impression we'd been hoping to make!

> "There's absolutely nothing that wipes the smile off a comedian's face faster than somebody ripping his house apart."

We waited till Tracy went out for a few hours and tried to get it all done and fixed before he came home, none the wiser. As Wayde noted, "There's absolutely nothing that wipes the smile off a comedian's face faster than somebody ripping his house apart."

Luckily we got everything inside and the front door restored to normal without our celebrity client ever catching on. Once all of the fiberglass panels made it into the basement, we used gel coating to seal them up. But then the complex filtration system wouldn't fit in the equipment room

set aside to house the tank's support system, so we had to improvise a new spot for it. All of that while managing the process of filling the tank with three hundred boxes of nutrient-enriched seawater containing naturally occurring beneficial bacteria and 1,500 pounds of live sand, both of which would allow the tank to become safely inhabitable much faster than if we used untreated tap water and an inert substrate.

Normally we thoroughly test all of our aquariums for potential leaks before they ever leave the manufacturing facility, but in this case, since it had to be transported in pieces and assembled on site, there was no chance to subject the shark tank to such scrutiny. We just had to fill it up and take our chances. Any small mistake or misalignment spelled certain disaster.

"I hope Tracy's homeowner insurance covers leaking shark tanks," Brett joked, though in the end the tank held up perfectly.

We also had some trouble getting the rays into the aquarium, a process that Wayde compared to trying to grab a moving string of barbed wire (because of the rays' sharp spines and the spiky thorns on the ends of their tails). But careful handling meant that every one of them made it in without incident. From there, the rest of the installation went along as smoothly as a shark swimming through deep waters. More importantly, Tracy Morgan couldn't have been more impressed.

"You dudes take it to ten!" he said with unbridled enthusiasm. "This is a joy, to have these creatures from the sea in my own home. From now on, here in my basement, every week is Shark Week!"

What You Didn't See on TV

Of all our clients—celebrity or otherwise—Tracy Morgan probably spends the most time obsessing over his aquariums and the organisms living inside them. He wants all the marine life in his care to have the best home possible, and he really tries to get into their heads and hearts to make sure that's happening. Tracy's not just a hobbyist; he's interested in promoting aquariums as a fun, educational pastime, which means a lot to all of us. He may act silly on television, but he's very serious about his tanks—just like us!

Featured Fish
Green Moray Eel
Seen in: Tracy Morgan Shark Tank

Channeling his *30 Rock* character's personal goal of "living every week like it's Shark Week," comedic actor extraordinaire Tracy Morgan challenged ATM to build him an unbelievable shark tank for his very own home. Featuring blacktip, whitetip, and sand sharks, the results totally blew him out of the water. But a top-flight aquarium does not live on sharks alone, so Brett and Wayde also included a green moray eel (*Gymnothorax funebris*) capable of growing up to 8 feet in length!

Native to the Caribbean, with an aggressive temperament that makes them fit to live alongside all of those sharks, this species requires a tank of no less than 500 gallons, and is not for the beginning or even moderately experienced aquarist, as this potentially dangerous breed can inflict severe bites on a careless tender during feeding, or even escape entirely from a poorly secured tank.

NEIL PATRICK HARRIS AND THE MAGIC CASTLE

SPECIFICATIONS

Dimensions: 48" H x 34" W x 34" D

Volume: 240 gallons / freshwater

Episode Name: Love Is an Illusion

Airdate: September 15, 2012

An acclaimed star of stage and screen who got his start as a child actor, Neil Patrick Harris has been a dedicated magician since his teenage years. Named one of *Time* magazine's 100 Most Influential People in 2010, he's got his own star on the Hollywood Walk of Fame and has hosted the Tony Awards on Broadway multiple times, but no accolade has meant more to him than mastering the craft of magic sufficiently to serve as head of the Board of Directors for the prestigious Academy of Magical Arts.

Founded in 1952 to develop and promote of the art of magic, the Academy maintains a private clubhouse at the famed Magic Castle in Los Angeles that houses their world-famous collection of artifacts and memorabilia. "It's the coolest hobby in the world," Harris gushed while giving us a private tour of the Academy's hallowed inner sanctum. "So I want the most magical tank you've ever built."

The star of *Doogie Howser, M.D.; How I Met Your Mother;* and the Harold and Kumar franchise knew he wanted something to fit with the Magic Castle's upscale decor and enhance its appeal as a place of mystery, illusion, and wonder, but he left the exact details up to us. Eventually, inspired by the surroundings, Brett hit upon the idea of re-creating one of famed escape artist Harry Houdini's most memorable performances: He hung upside-down in a "water torture cell" while confined in a straitjacket and chains . . . and then escaped! To make a lifelike rendering of the world's most famous magician, we hired a top Hollywood effects company to create a Houdini

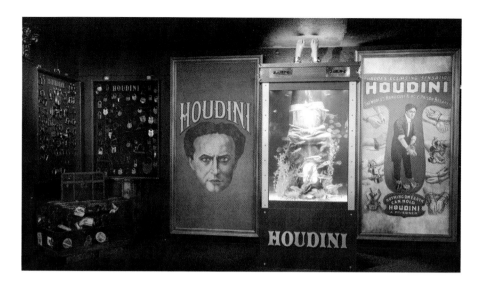

mannequin complete with waterproof face paint and synthetic hair capable of withstanding life inside an aquarium. Then we tracked down an authentic Houdini-era straitjacket at a magic shop in Vegas.

A former amateur magician himself, the General insisted on tagging along for that trip and reunited with some old friends hanging around the magic shop. Intent on impressing Brett and Wayde, he had them tie him up in the straitjacket to make sure it worked and then swore he could free himself from it without any help. Unfortunately, after ten minutes of trying (and failing), he remained as tightly confined as when he began.

"Don't feel bad," Brett assured his father. "I couldn't get out of that thing either."

"You couldn't get *into* this thing," the General replied, as we led him out of the store, still stuck in the straitjacket like a mental patient.

Meanwhile, back at ATM headquarters, Robbie the Redneck and the design team set to work on building the tank, including fitting the mannequin with a special filtration tube to create the illusion of underwater

> The tank draws gasps of wonder from all who peer into it, from the Academy's junior members to those old enough to have seen the great escape artist perform live and in person.

breathing when bubbles rise from Houdini's mouth. Once the "water tor-ture cell" was fully installed, we filled it with red tail and vampire barra-cudas, spotted metynnis, a swamp eel, and a rare blue-eyed plexico, each selected to look menacing and add to the scene's drama and suspense.

Now one of the most popular attractions on the official Magic Castle tour, the tank draws gasps of wonder from the Academy's junior members to those old enough to have seen the great escape artist perform in person. As for ATM's famous client, he couldn't be happier.

"It's perfect, it's phenomenal," Neil Patrick Harris declared. "The spirit of Houdini lives on in this tank!"

What You Didn't See on TV

Until we got to the Magic Castle, we had no idea that Neil Patrick Harris was a bona fide magician. He gave us a little demo that showed just how skilled he is at the art of illusion. Also, it's hard to see on TV just how much he loves aquariums, but he really appreciates them and knows a lot about how they work—and he watches the show!

CHILDREN'S HOSPITAL TREASURE CHEST TANK

SPECIFICATIONS

Dimensions: 36" H x 96" W x 42" D

Volume: 625 gallons / saltwater

Episode Name: Midwest Zest

Airdate: November 17, 2012

In Detroit, where they started out as a small mom-and-pop pizza restaurant in 1959, Little Caesar's works closely with the Children's Hospital of Michigan Foundation to give something back to the community that's done so much to support their now global business. Still owned by the Ilitch family, who sold the chain's first pie, Little Caesar's decided to fund the installation of a custom aquarium near the hospital's cafeteria, where the most children would see it.

"If there's anything I love more than fish, it's pizza," Wayde joked, while helping himself to a slice during an early strategy session. We knew the tank needed an uplifting theme that conveyed hope, healing, and better days ahead. The aquarium had to be fun, even though the responsibility we took in building it was very serious. After all, what kind of custom job could ever be more important to get just right than this one?

> "If there's anything I love more than fish, it's pizza."

With input from the president of the hospital, we decided on a treasure chest theme, with pieces of gold pizza inside the chest to represent Little Caesar's, plus orange fish the color of their logo. Then we returned to Las Vegas to work out the details of a tricky build. The tank not only needed to be tilted in the front and back but also tapered up front so the treasure chest appeared to be perpetually overflowing.

In exchange for all of this extra work, Robbie the Redneck made one small request: pizza . . . and lots of it. He practically lives in a trailer behind the ATM production facility so he can work all the overtime required to keep up with Wayde's ambition and Brett's visions, so it's no wonder that the subsequent care package from Little Caesar's soon served as breakfast, lunch, and dinner. At one point he even heated up his leftover pizza on the hood of Brett's car!

"Don't mess with another man's vehicle," Brett cried in indignation. Then he hatched a plan for revenge. He and Brett waited for Redneck to fall asleep before hooking up his trailer and dragging him out into the middle of the desert. After hiding in his own car all night, Brett witnessed Robbie's priceless reaction to finding himself literally in the middle of nowhere.

"That shows some real dedication to pranking," Brett boasted.

"If only pranks were your job," Wayde shot back.

Next stop: Exotic Reef Imports to source some clown fish to match Little Caesars' orange logo, plus gold flake fish and copper band butterflies to represent buried treasure. Then off to Detroit, where we soon discovered that the tank wouldn't fit in the hospital's elevator. That meant bringing it in on the other side of the building, balancing all 20 square feet of fragile acrylic on forklifts, and wheeling it into position. But it turned out that

there had been a miscommunication with the hospital. All the plumbing for the tank, already assembled back in Las Vegas, had to be taken apart and completely rebuilt on site.

"Yeah, baby!" Wayde exclaimed when the moment of truth arrived and it all came together like clockwork. "I never thought I'd be so excited about plumbing."

Fully installed, the tank holds 750 gallons of water and weighs over 25 tons. Inside, over one hundred schooling fish glimmer like gold, plus two yellow tangs, a blue hippo, two butterflies, chromis, green birds, harlequin tusk, clown fish, flame angels, and speckled angels. We even found pajama cardinals that look like swimming pepperonis to fit the pizza theme.

"This is a one-of-a-kind hospital," the president told us, "and now we've got a one-of-a-kind tank to go with it. The kids are gonna love it!"—and they do.

What You Didn't See on TV

We struggled a lot trying to coat the coins and get the statue exactly right, but putting this tank together on location—rather than back at ATM's production facility—presented the biggest challenge. We always do whatever it takes to make things work, but it's always easier to work things out back at the shop first!

Featured Fish
Blue Hippo Tang
Seen in: Children's Hospital Treasure Chest Tank

Nobody in the aquarium industry will ever forget the public's incredible reaction when the Pixar animated classic *Finding Nemo* came out in 2003. Literally millions of children and adults—inspired by the tale of a brave little clown fish who went on an unexpected and epic adventure—set up aquariums of their own, including their very own clown fish of course.

With the sequel, *Finding Dory,* set for release in 2016, we can expect a similar phenomenon, only this time the title character and main attraction will be Marlin's friend and traveling companion, an adorable blue hippo tang (*Paracanthurus hepatus*). A brightly hued species of Indo-Pacific surgeonfish long popular among tropical aquarium enthusiasts, it's unfortunately much more fragile to keep than a clown fish, requiring more specialized care and a larger tank (at least 180 gallons). They also have a sharp spine that they will extend when threatened or excited. Native to Kenya, they can grow up to one foot in length in captivity, preferring water between 72 and 78 degrees and an herbivore's diet of algae, seaweed, and prepared fish food.

JACKASS PRANK TANK

SPECIFICATIONS

Dimensions: 60" H x 120" W x 36" D

Volume: 1,120 gallons / saltwater

Episode Name: Pranks and Dranks!

Airdate: March 22, 2013

From the first moment Brett learned that *Jackass* producer Jeff Tremaine wanted a new aquarium, he knew that ATM had to land the gig. After all, *Jackass* and *Tanked* both share a serious love of good-natured pranking and going way over the top—though nothing at the ATM office will ever approach the extreme lunacy of *Jackass*'s legendary stunts and ill-advised competitions.

Brett lying down on the job . . . to get the job done

"When it comes to practical jokes, we may have met our match this time," Brett admitted.

During a consultation with Jeff in his self-described "man-room," where he planned to install the new aquarium, we learned that our latest showbiz client kept tanks his whole life and wanted a special one dedicated to celebrating *Jackass*'s ten-year anniversary. He even had the fish for it picked out. All we had to do was follow him out the pool, and we could see for ourselves.

When we got there, however, there were no exotic fish—just Wee-man and Pontius dressed as mermaids and having a swim.

"I'm getting to work with two of my favorite jackasses!" Brett cried in delight.

"I'm lucky enough to work with my favorite jackass every day," Wayde replied.

Getting down to business, Jeff asked for a 3-D rendering of the world-famous *Jackass* skull to be submerged inside his custom tank. "That logo means the world to me. I don't like it to be cartoony, so make it exact. Otherwise, I love what you guys do, so just do your thing. Though, believe

Unveiling the tank to Johnny Knoxville and Chris Pontius

it or not, I want it a little toned down. With realistic reef work, raw steel, and reclaimed wood panels."

> Frankie from the sales department learned the hard way that shopping carts don't have brakes, and he ended up in the hospital.

Back in Las Vegas, we decided to ignore the warning at the beginning of the prank show and re-create one of the most famous stunts ever attempted: racing down a steep hill in a shopping cart. Wayde stepped up to go first . . . until Heather caught him in the act and put a stop to that immediately. Lucky for him that she did, too, because Frankie from the sales department learned the hard way that shopping carts don't have brakes, and he ended up in the hospital.

Meanwhile, we decided to incorporate a trick keg tap into the aquarium, which, when pulled, instead of dispensing ice-cold beer would open a hidden compartment from which a coiled boxing glove burst forth to greet its unsuspecting victims with a punch to the groin. The glove works by pneumatically triggering a compressor with settings ranging from "Humiliate" to "Hospitalize."

Knoxville gives the prank kegerator a try . . .

The tank itself reaches from floor to ceiling with 2-inch-thick bulletproof acrylic walls and sixty fish in residence—diverse species from all over the world. Custom wood panels and a canopy gave it a sleek look while handmade coral re-created the *Jackass* logo and of course a shopping cart, in honor of the iconic stunt.

When it came to stocking the aquarium, Jeff had some very specific ideas about what he wanted, so he tagged along with us on our next trip to Exotic Reef Imports. None of his previous visits to the local pet store prepared him for entering the 100,000-gallon headquarters of one of the world's leading wholesale fish suppliers, though.

"This is blowing my mind," Jeff admitted on arrival before setting out to find an ideal eel for his tank. After consulting with one of the on-staff experts, he picked a leopard eel along with an assortment of fish like Picasso triggers and unicorn tangs that can live in harmony with eels. Plus, in accordance with *Jackass*'s reputation for boldness, they're both visually striking breeds: The Picassos look like bright, floating brush-strokes, and the unicorns, which can live ten years in a tank, grow horns on their heads.

By the end of the process, Jeff had been so hands-on with his aquarium that he learned how to bag his own fish for the trip home, where, if everything went according to plan, his custom tank would be waiting. Though, as usual, it wouldn't be easy.

Our behind-the-scenes hero, Robbie "the Redneck" drove the entire aquarium, already assembled, from Las Vegas into the Hollywood Hills, where he had to wind his way slowly up steep, narrow, twisting streets that quickly backed up with a long line of luxury vehicles honking madly. It was among the most stressful moments of a stressful job.

But the payoff couldn't have been greater. When Jeff saw the entire aquarium assembled, he declared: "You guys killed it, man!" Then *Jackass* star Johnny Knoxville showed up unexpectedly and got suckered into pulling the trick beer tap—with a quick punch in the groin as his reward.

Gotcha, Knoxville!

What You Didn't See on TV

We already knew Jeff Tremaine. We had met him in Raleigh, North Carolina, when he was filming Bad Grandpa and we were installing a sushi- and burger-themed tank ("Nigiri and the NBA" episode) in a restaurant called The Cowfish. We had dinner together, hit it off, and have been friends ever since.

Featured Fish
Picasso Triggerfish
Seen in: *Jackass* **Prank Tank**

Easily identified by its distinctly whimsical blue, black, and yellow modern art–like markings, the Picasso triggerfish (*Rhinecanthus aculeatus*) is relatively easy to take care of despite its aggressive tendencies when kept in a fish tank. It does require a fairly large 180-gallon aquarium, minimum, though preferably with a plethora of rocks and caves where it can hide out occasionally. Also, don't be surprised if this species starts to rearrange its environment to suit its own needs while making its distinctive growling sound. Native to Tahiti, they grow to a maximum of 10 inches in an aquarium and prefer water temps between 72 and 78 degrees Fahrenheit. Carnivores, they thrive on a diet of varied meaty treats like clams, squid, krill, small fish, and hard-shelled shrimp.

Tanks and Pranks

Aside from building amazing aquariums, there's nothing the ATM team loves more than playing good-natured pranks on one another, a tradition that started long before the cameras ever started rolling. Every fan of the show has a favorite prank, and naturally so do the pranksters themselves.

Wayde

My favorite was the time we convinced Frankie and the General that they were heading to a client's house for a consultation and had them dress up in suits. Before they left, though, we filled the A/C vents in their car with baby powder and set the fan to high. As soon as the engine started, powder blew all over them. One for the history books!

Brett

Before we started filming *Tanked,* Wayde was always the prankster at ATM. Once I realized that pranks were going to play a big part in the show, I did some serious research on the Internet to make sure that I could give as good as I got. Since then, I've never missed an opportunity to make everyone laugh with a timely prank. That's why tricking Wayde into eating all of that hot sauce after he tricked me with the fake lottery tickets is my favorite. The idea originated when I was on spring break in my twenties and did it to all of my friends in Acapulco. It was such sweet revenge for me and such a spicy comeuppance for Wayde!

Heather

Agnes helped me get back at Brett for giving me insanely spicy popcorn. I taped a plastic sheet to his door and filled it almost full with popcorn. When Brett opened the door, popcorn poured all over him and into his office. Steaming mad, he slammed the door shut and locked himself inside his office—

with all those pieces of popcorn everywhere. He was screaming and yelling; it was hysterical. Talk about a good prank getting even better! I do love paybacks.

Irwin

I used Wayde's phony lotto tickets to help him fool Brett into thinking he'd won $10,000. Oh the look on Brett's face when he finally realized that he hadn't won any money. Then he took his revenge on Wayde—and not me—by tricking him into eating a sandwich drenched in hot sauce and washing it down with hot-sauce-laced soda!

Robbie

The best prank never made it on the show. The production team was taking a break from filming, and I had a key to the trailer behind the shop that they use as their offices. I broke in and booby trapped the place with a bunch of stink bombs, so every time they sat down the whole place stank to high heaven!

Agnes

My favorite prank—of *many* contenders—was when Brett smeared the inside of a phone handle with black grease and told Wayde that he had a call. I had no idea what Brett was up to, so, when Wayde hung up the phone and had black grease all over his face, I nearly lost it. I laughed until my sides hurt. What you didn't see on the show was that black mascara had smeared all over my face from the tears because I was laughing so hard!

TOP HAT KOI TANK

SPECIFICATIONS

Dimensions: 34"H x 72" diameter

Volume: 600 gallons / freshwater

Episode Name: Tip of the Hat to the Devils

Airdate: April 12, 2013

For more than twenty years, the D Bar J Hat Company of Las Vegas has made custom caps for customers from all over the globe. Head head-dresser David Johnson started out reshaping worn-out cowboy hats for his fellow teammates on a competitive country-western dance team and learned as he went. Eventually he turned reviving a few "old favorites that needed some tending" into his own thriving business.

All that time on the road, learning the details of restoring hats of all shapes, styles, and eras—even back into the 1800s—paid off. Johnson built up an expert's knowledge of the art and craft of hatmaking, filling custom orders for celebrities like Clint Black and Tony Curtis.

Naturally all of his employees dress the part.

"These guys look like they just stepped out of a time machine," Wayde said of the Old West vibe of the D Bar J store. The newly renovated hat space included not just the retail operation but also an event space to host dance lessons and live entertainment. All that was missing was the planned centerpiece: an ATM aquarium. David Johnson wanted an indoor koi pond shaped like a top hat with a flat brim to serve as a circular bar around the tank, and of course he wanted old hats inside the tank, which presented a challenge since the materials

Koi in the wild

in the hats could break down in the water and harm the fish. We had to coat them carefully first with a non-toxic putty called polygon—oh, and it all had to be done in two weeks!

Feeling the heat of that deadline, we headed back to the manufacturing facility immediately, where we drew up plans for a cylindrical tank with 360-degree views and a flare-out canopy on top to disguise the lighting system. Then we wrapped a bar around the bottom of the tank to re-create the brim before tying it all together with a beautiful ribbon—just like the finest hats in the showroom.

To track down the exotic koi for inside the tank, we relied on Segrest Farms in Florida, one of the world's largest wholesale fish distributors and our go-to operation for anything freshwater. After consulting the experts, we acquired six-month-old, 8-inch butterfly, called that because their pectoral fins stretch out like butterfly wings. Segrest had the butterflies flown in from the Far East, where they grow quickly in warm water.

"Koi have been bred for centuries to bring out their beautiful colors and markings," Wayde noted. "In Asia, they have koi shows like we have dog shows here."

After a few setbacks and some fancy footwork, we had to work nearly nonstop right up until the moment of the big unveiling, all part of the new store's grand opening celebration.

"If we don't get this done in time, their grand opening's going to be a bland opening," Wayde kidded.

As time ticked down, Wayde and Brett let the koi, still in their shipping bags, float on top of the empty tank to get used to the temperature. Then they washed each fish in an isolated bucket before introducing it to the aquarium. After two weeks of incredibly hard work, there was barely time to catch a breath before the top hat tank's big moment.

Fortunately, when he saw it for the first time, Johnson doffed his hat in appreciation before celebrating the arrival of his store's centerpiece in the most appropriate manner possible.

"I've been at this a long time," Brett said, "and this is the first time I showed a client their tank and they were so happy they started dancing!"

> "This is the first time I showed a client their tank and they were so happy they started dancing!"

What You Didn't See on TV

D Bar J had everything there to make hats from scratch, just like back in the days of the Old Wild West, including really cool machines to stretch the hats until they fit perfectly.

SODA POP ROCKET SHIP TANK

SPECIFICATIONS

Dimensions: 48" H x 48" W x 24" D

Volume: 190 gallons / saltwater

Episode Name: Spin the Bottles

Airdate: April 19, 2013

At the flagship Rocket Fizz Soda Pop and Candy Shop in Camarillo, California, you can take a nostalgic trip back to the era of the neighborhood soda fountain, including your choice from among thousands of bottled soda pops in every flavor imaginable. Created by Rocket Fizz founders and company owners Rob Powells and Ryan Morgan, the franchise has forty locations spanning ten different states.

"We're all about American nostalgia and bringing back the past," "Rocket" Rob explained when we visited the shop for a consultation. "We built our stores around old-fashioned candy and old-fashioned sodas."

To get his creative juices flowing, Brett sampled one of the more exotic offerings in the shop: a bacon-flavored soda. He looked a little trepidatious bringing the bottle to his lips, but he broke into a wide grin and proclaimed that all he needed was a side of pancakes to complete the meal. Meanwhile, Wayde wanted to indulge his own sweet tooth a little—again, all in the name of research.

Stocking the rocket ship tank with soda bottles

TANKED

"I'm like a kid in a candy store," Wayde gushed.

"You're like *three* kids in a candy store!" Brett snarked back.

"Rocket" Rob explained that he treasured his childhood fish tank, so installing a completely customized one in the store felt like a perfect fit. But it had to be tall with a small footprint because floor space was limited and the store needed to maximize room for displaying candy, merchandise, and soda bottles.

Picturing a tall, curved tank, Brett immediately had one of his visions, this time a rock ship preparing for liftoff. He figured it could be built as a half

cylinder pushed up against the wall, with some kind of count down, light show, and fog blastoff.

"Kids will come in here and go nuts!" he exclaimed before promising that the sides of the spaceship would have shelves to display product. With all the plumbing, a fog machine hidden beneath the support stand, and a rocket nose on top, it would look perfect. We added a special air line so it appeared as if the soda bottles inside the tank were constantly bubbling, and hidden speakers announced the official launch countdown.

Meanwhile, we had to figure out how to fill the

rocket's tall, narrow tank. At Exotic Reef Imports, Brett gave the supplier a good idea of the theme. "Rocket Fizz is all about bright colors and crazy flavors, so the fish that we pick out gotta be extra sweet!"

What could fit that theme better than a cinnamon clown fish? It can be aggressive if taken from the wild, but it displays much tamer behavior when captive bred, forming peaceful schools of five or six inside a well-maintained tank. We also added lemonpeel fish, blue faced angels that grow more colorful with age, whimsical sharp-nose puffers, and, to keep everything clean, a goat fish, which uses two prongs to sift through the sand looking for tiny morsels of food.

To top it all off, we created a special command center with working buttons and dials to control the rocket's launch sequence like a real piece of NASA equipment.

"This tank is real Americana, just like the 1950s," Rob declared upon witnessing the blastoff sequence for the first time. "It's exactly what our stores are all about. Everything that is our brand is literally in this fish tank."

Weeks later, his business partner confirmed that their enthusiasm for the aquarium only grew stronger as it became a featured attraction in their flagship store. "We didn't realize how popular *Tanked* was until we did this," Ryan Morgan told the local *Camarillo Acorn* newspaper. "It was like the whole town knew who they were."

What You Didn't See on TV

We sampled an *unbelievable* number of different flavored sodas. That was the first time Wayde had ever tried an unusually flavored soda, and his favorite was green apple. Everyone really did feel like a kid in a candy shop.

Featured Fish
Lemonpeel Angelfish
Seen in: Soda Pop Rocket Ship

The lemonpeel angelfish (*Centropyge flavissima*) features bright yellow coloring with sky-blue highlights around the eyes, lips, and at the tips of its fins, a vibrant look that really pops inside a fish tank. Capable of growing up to 6 inches long, it prefers water between 72 and 78 degrees Fahrenheit and needs to live in a tank of at least 70 gallons to stay happy and healthy in captivity, preferably with plenty of places to hide, like live rocks covered in beneficial microalgae.

Native to Fiji, they're omnivorous fish whose diet should include spirulina, marine algae, breed-specific prepared foods, frozen shrimp, and seaweed.

DUNKIN' DONUTS TANK

SPECIFICATIONS

Dimensions: 18" H x 36" diameter, turned on its side

Volume: 150 gallons / saltwater

Episode Name: Fermenting Donuts

Airdate: May 10, 2013

When Steve Rubiano, owner of a Dunkin' Donuts franchise in Riviera Beach, Florida, reached out to us about a custom aquarium for his business, Brett had some serious reservations—not about the client but about the wisdom of letting Wayde get too close to one of his favorite indulgences.

"Bringing Wayde here is a little dangerous," Brett said as the *Tanked* team made the initial on-site visit to the doughnut shop. "This is like taking a monkey to the banana farm!"

After so many years of intense research into this particularly delicious product line, Wayde did look a little disappointed when the Dunkin' Donuts owner wanted to talk about glass versus acrylic aquariums rather than jelly versus glazed doughnuts.

Even though it was for his small business, Steve wanted to go big on his aquarium, giving customers a thrill they'd never forget as well as a reason to return often and bring friends. "We want a tank that people will take pictures in front of," he explained, "something huge that gives them a real experience."

Maybe he was just hungry, but Wayde went for the obvious—a tank in the shape of a doughnut—even when Brett pointed out how difficult it would be to create properly. Taking a page from Brett's book, Wayde went one step further and suggested having the doughnut

> Wayde did look a little disappointed when the Dunkin' Donuts owner wanted to talk about glass versus acrylic aquariums rather than jelly versus glazed doughnuts.

dunked into an old fashioned saucer and cup. It was a strange role-reversal: Wayde was following his wildest vision wherever it led, and Brett was following after him, worrying over the real-world concerns of making it all work.

We started by bending acrylic on a compound bow until it formed a cylinder with a hole in the middle. Then we wrapped a fiberglass covering around the tank to smooth the acrylic's hard edges. The cup, meanwhile, was designed to hide the tank's pumps, filters, and plumbing.

To stock the tank, we chose fish that look like sprinkles and other tasty treats, starting with a chocolate tang, for obvious reasons, plus a fairy wrasse in rainbow colors, a boxfish, and several purple tao goby fish, which love to jump. When we arrived in Florida for the install, however, one of the three parts of the stand failed to arrive, holding up production completely. Brett called his dad, the General, to sort out the mess and get things moving again, which required tracking the missing package, postponing the live fish delivery, and changing the road crew's flights, hotel reservations, and car rentals—all at the last minute.

On the plus side, though, with literally nothing to do until the missing part arrived, Wayde took the opportunity to cross a line item off his bucket list: an airboat ride through the Everglades. Despite a few close encounters of the alligator kind, the airboat tour turned out to be even more enjoyable than expected, and the next morning the rest of the stand arrived.

"Time to make the doughnuts," Brett said, first thing.

With every piece accounted for, assembly of the aquarium went off without a hitch, including a custom LED light system with remote control of over 1,200 different colors and functions. Best of all, its proud new owner couldn't have been happier. "The tank's beautiful," Steve told the *Tanked* cameras. "This was my first time working with a TV show, and it was such a fun experience. Wayde and Brett are just two regular guys who love what they do. They're really funny, and we worked very well together."

What You Didn't See on TV

While taking a break, Wayde ate a bunch of free doughnuts, which gave him a serious sugar rush. He was talking a mile a minute and it looked like he was freaking out. Needless to say, he wasn't too upset that those shots didn't air.

JOHNNIE WALKER RV TANK

SPECIFICATIONS

Dimensions: 30" H x 80" W x 53" D

Volume: 354 gallons / saltwater

Episode name: Jurassic Campground

Airdate: May 31, 2013

Not to be confused with the famous blended scotch, Johnnie Walker RV is Nevada's leading dealer of recreational vehicles. Family owned and operated since 1963, they've served the local community for four generations, employing a friendly and knowledgeable sales staff, stocking only quality vehicles and parts, and offering dependable service and secure financing.

Since he practically lives in an RV parked behind the ATM production facility while working on his most complex creations, Robbie "the Redneck" took an understandably personal interest in this particular job . . . particularly when Michael Walker, current company owner, challenged us to transform a camper into a rolling aquarium capable of getting hitched up and pulled across the country in celebration of the business's 50th anniversary.

Redneck loved the idea. Not everyone on the ATM staff shared his enthusiasm.

"I've been worried things would head in this direction," Wayde admitted, clearly concerned. "We've done cars and even a small bus . . . but, man, an *RV*?"

> Not everyone on the ATM staff shared Redneck's enthusiasm.

Matters got even more fraught with peril when the Johnnie Walker management team announced that they'd already picked out a 12-foot RV camper to retrofit with tanks—an Econ trailer furnished by Pacific Coachworks—all without any input from us. No wonder Wayde made an executive decision to delegate the entire project to Redneck as part of a general effort to lower his overall stress level. Luckily, Redneck gladly

accepted the responsibility, which offered him a chance to work on his dream tank without undue interference.

The first major challenge involved figuring how to reduce the weight of the aquarium so the RV wouldn't collapse once it was installed. Making the tanks in a U-shape decreased their water volume significantly while simultaneously offering a unique view. But Redneck had to figure out how to get the tanks and all the stands and plumbing inside the camper without tearing it apart.

"I've slept in trailers many times, I've even lived in trailers, but I've never taken one apart before," he lamented when faced with the daunting prospect.

Fortunately, Johnnie Walker's headquarters lay just around the corner from our production facility, and some bona fide RV experts made a house call to help out. While they carefully removed the front of the trailer, Redneck took a break and test-drove his pick of the best RVs on the lot. Wayde the workaholic showed that he can't delegate all that well by snooping around the project as much as possible, even spying on Redneck via ATM security cameras.

The view from inside the RV

Wayde still got to pick the fish for this special anniversary aquarium—otherwise he might have gone completely stir crazy! At Exotic Reef Imports, he and Brett decided on a cross-country road-trip theme, which meant filling the tank with species indigenous to the Atlantic, Pacific, and Gulf Coast, including high fin snappers, purple Spanish hogs, red and yellow Cuban hogs, blue chromis, spade fish, and, last but not least, a huge dog-faced puffer.

Just before the unveiling, Redneck and the rest of the *Tanked* team admitted that it had been nerve-wracking to see the camper ripped apart before their eyes, but we all agreed that the end result spoke for itself, right down to the little touches inside the tank, which fleshed out its road-trip theme, like sticks with marshmallows on the end and a camping lantern coated in luminescent paint so it glowed in the dark.

"This aquarium, custom-built for our family, definitely surpasses anything that we could have envisioned," said Michael Walker, marketing director for Johnnie Walker RVs and great-grandson of the company's founder. "We are honored to be the first RV business to be featured on *Tanked*! What a great way to celebrate fifty years of our family's business."

What You Didn't See on TV

We had to cut off the whole front nose of the RV to get the tank in. There was a little of that on the show, but getting that done proved a lot more involved than what you saw. It was a particularly tough build because RVs are a little too thin and lightweight to support the weight of a full tank and a stand.

Featured Fish
Blue Reef Chromis
Seen in: Johnnie Walker RV Tank

Native to the warm, tranquil waters of the Caribbean, the blue reef chromis (*Chromis cyaneus*), an active fish, spends most of its time swimming around in the upper part of an aquarium. It even encourages other species to move out from under rocks and behind hiding places, making them a welcome addition to any tank. Reaching a maximum length of 5 inches in captivity, these omnivores can live happily in just 30 gallons of water, feeding on everything from meaty treats to flaked food and frozen preparations.

Known as shoaling fish—meaning they group together for social reasons without necessarily forming tight, coordinated packs like schooling fish—they should be kept in small groups rather than left alone in a tank without companions of their own species.

SCOTTISH MONSTER TANK

Never Seen on TV!

SPECIFICATIONS

Dimensions: 35' H x 11' diameter

Volume: 25,000 gallons / saltwater

In a house adjacent to one of the most famous golf courses in the world, ATM installed a 32-foot-tall cylindrical aquarium that starts in the basement next to the pool and extends up to the fourth-floor master bedroom.

The house, built alongside the Gleneagles Golf Course in Perthshire, Scotland, literally had to be constructed around the massive tank, which stands so tall that performing routine maintenance requires climbing up to the roof of the building.

Wayde called it the most difficult installation of his career. "We went all the way to the UK to crane a massive, 11-foot-diameter, 4-story-tall tank into the foundation of this guy's house in the cold and rain. We also had to build a separate filtration room to support something that big

and assemble the coral inserts on site. Plus, in Scotland, they have different power and different equipment than we're used to back home, different tools to fit different size piping. Overseas you have to deal with customs, where one little T not crossed can hold up a whole shipment, meaning lots of workers end up getting paid to stand around. Stuff that I can get done at home with a quick phone call, like garbage removal, suddenly isn't so easy once you're overseas."

Despite those challenges, the installation went swimmingly, and the aquarium remains a stunning part of the home today. Too bad it all happened before the *Tanked* cameras ever started rolling. It would have made for a classic episode of the show—particularly if Brett tried out a Scottish accent.

PUBLIC ATM TANKS

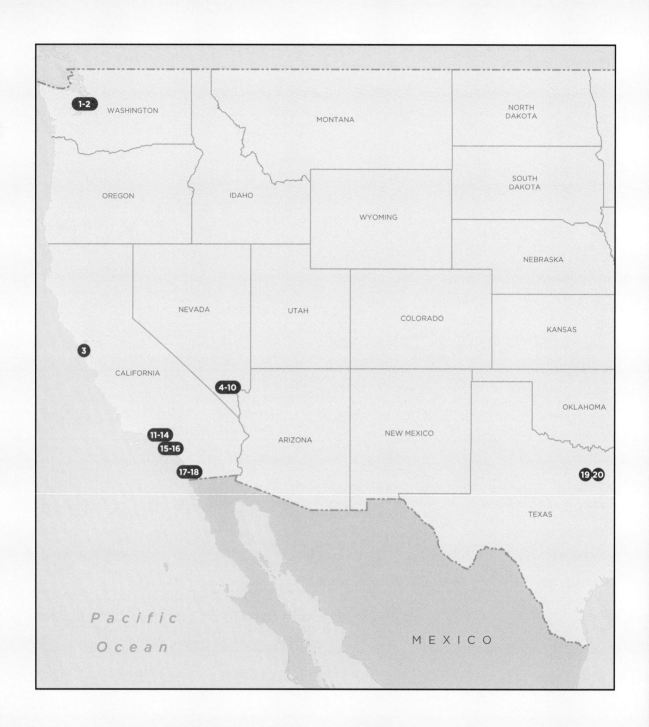

1 Giant Pacific Octopus Tank
 Seattle Aquarium
 Seattle, WA
 SeattleAquarium.org

2 Jellyfish Tank
 Seattle Aquarium
 Seattle, WA
 SeattleAquarium.org

3 California Academy of Sciences
San Francisco, CA
CalAcademy.org

4 Bejing Noodle 9
Caesars Palace
Las Vegas, NV
CaesarsPalace.com

5 Black Spade Tattoo
Las Vegas, NV
BlackSpadeTattoo.com

6 Halloween Mart
Las Vegas, NV
HalloweenMart.com

7 Johnnie Walker RV
Las Vegas, NV
JohnnieWalkerRV.com

8 Popcorn Girl
Las Vegas, NV
PopcornGirlVegas.com

9 Silverton Casino
Las Vegas, NV
SilvertonCasino.com

10 Vegas Weddings
Las Vegas, NV
702wedding.com

11 Camp Oaks
Ojai, CA
OaksSpa.com

12 Rocket Fizz
Camarillo, CA
RocketFizz.com

13 Malibu Family Wines
Malibu, CA
MalibuFamilyWines.com

14 Malibu Lumber Yard
Malibu, CA
TheMalibuLumberYard.com

15 California Science Center
Los Angeles, CA
CaliforniaScienceCenter.org

16 Bella Terra
Huntington Beach, CA
ResidencesBellaTerra.com

17 Pizza Port
San Diego, CA
PizzaPort.com

18 Valley View Casino
San Diego, CA
ValleyViewCasino.com

19 Museum of Living Art
Fort Worth Zoo
Fort Worth, TX
FortWorthZoo.org

20 IBOC Mega Church
Dallas, TX
IBOCChurch.org

1 **Minneapolis Zoo**
Minneapolis, MN
MNZoo.com

2 **Real-Time Leasing**
Eagan, MN
RealTimeLeasing.com

3 **Wave Tank**
Museum of Science and Industry
Chicago, IL
MSIChicago.org

4 **Children's Hospital of Michigan**
Detroit, MI
ChildrensDMC.org

5 **Night Hotel**
New York, NY
NightHotelNY.com

6 **Staten Island Ferry Terminal**
Staten Island, NY
SIFerry.com

7 **Applebee's Coney Island**
Brooklyn, NY
Applebees.com

8 **Plessers Appliances**
Babylon, NY
Plessers.com

9 **Polar Bear Exhibit**
Columbus Zoo
Columbus, OH
ColsZoo.com

10 **Nationwide Children's Hospital**
Columbus, OH
NationwideChildrens.com

11 **T-Rex Cafe**
Kansas City, MO
TRexCafe.com

12 **Cowfish Restaurant**
Raleigh, NC
TheCowfish.com

13 **Furnitureland South**
Raleigh, NC
FurniturelandSouth.com

14 **Grizzly Bear Exhibit**
Memphis Zoo
Memphis, TN
MemphisZoo.org

15 **Wind Creek Casino**
Atmore, AL
WindCreekAtmore.com

16 **Nails and Beyond**
The Villages, FL

17 **T-Rex Cafe**
Downtown Disney
Orlando, FL
TRexCafe.com

18 **Tropical Smoothie**
Tampa, FL
TropicalSmoothie.com

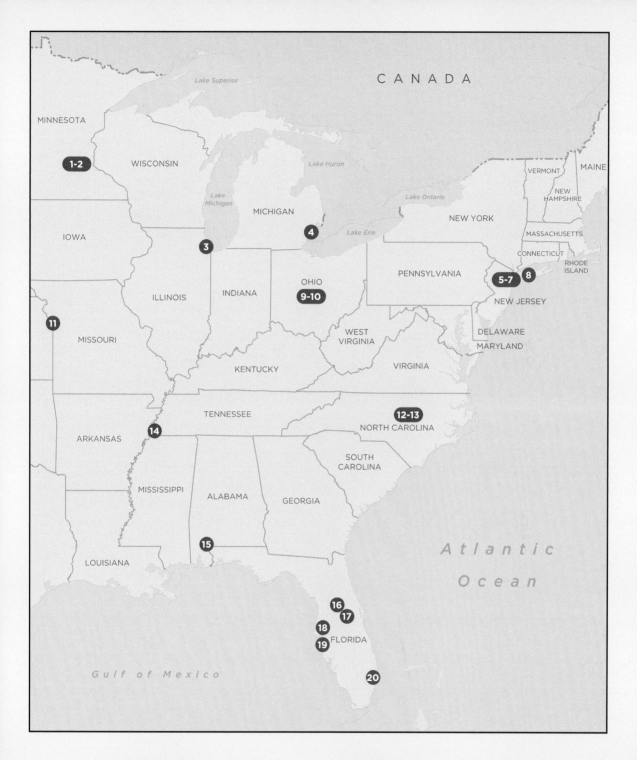

19 Selby Public Library
Sarasota, FL
SCGov.net/Library

20 Dunkin' Donuts
Riviera Beach, FL
DunkinDonuts.com

THE OFFICIAL ATM "GET STARTED" AQUARIUM GUIDE

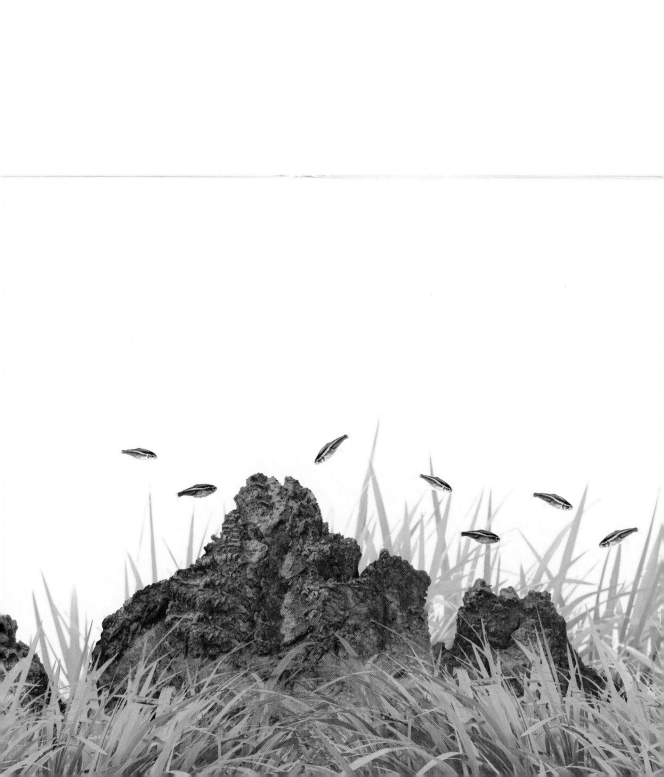

TRY THIS AT HOME!

The unparalleled beauty and tranquillity of a well-tended aquarium makes keeping fish among the most popular pastimes in the world today. But starting a tank isn't like collecting stamps or rare coins. As an aquarist you are dealing with live plants and animals, so you must take complete responsibility for their proper care.

Fish are, after all, no different from dogs, cats, or exotic birds: They must be treated with love and respect at all times by someone with a full understanding of their needs. If you don't have the time, interest, attention span, or resources to follow through, please don't start. Instead, go to your nearest public aquarium, where you can see a huge array of marine life and learn all about your favorite fish without making the major commitment that tending your own tank requires.

For the rest of us, the process begins with a lot of research and planning, so don't buy or borrow any costly equipment until you've carefully plotted out every aspect of how you will set up, stock, and maintain your aquarium. Take notes, draw sketches, create a to-do list, and carefully budget how much it will all cost, including feeding and maintenance going forward. Then find an expert—at a quality pet store, through a local aquarium society, or on one of the many excellent online forums devoted to the hobby—and together with your mentor form a step-by-step plan for building and filling your tank.

Remember, the information in this Official ATM Get Started Aquarium Guide is meant to do just that: help you get started and point you in the right direction. It covers most of the basic questions that you should ask before buying and assembling a tank, but you'll need to acquire a lot more knowledge to succeed—some of it as you go. In fact, constantly learning new things should be one of the most exciting parts of the fish tank experience.

Now let's begin your aquarium adventure!

Choosing an Aquarium

The size of the tank you choose will determine how many and what type of fish you can keep as well as their behavior once introduced into the aquarium. A good rule of thumb holds that to thrive in captivity, a fish requires 1 gallon of water for every inch of its length when full grown. This is based not on the size of the tank in gallons but on the amount of water inside. Keep in mind: A 10-gallon tank may hold only 7 gallons of water, the remaining space taken up by rocks, coral, plants, fish, decorations, and air at the top.

Never overcrowd your aquarium; that's one of the most common mistakes made by newbies. Also, remember, while the rule of thumb is helpful as a starting place, you have to study each fish as an individual before you add it to your tank. Lively swimmers need far more space than a more docile species of the same size.

Another common rookie mistake is believing that a smaller tank will be easier to maintain than a larger one. Exactly the opposite is true. As Wayde points out: "A small problem in a small tank is actually a big problem. But if you take that same problem and dilute it in a tank that's ten times as large, you'll have a much better chance to correct it before things get out of hand. That's why I recommend that kids start with at least a 50-gallon tank."

For most fish, the standard rectangular aquarium shape works well, but certain breeds like catfish and labyrinth fish need a wider, more shallow environment. The shape of your aquarium can also be custom designed based on where it will live in your home. Modern acrylic tanks like the ones we manufacture can be bent into any shape imaginable.

Cover

Most aquariums require a cover to keep dust and debris from collecting on the surface of the water. They also prevent fish from jumping out of the top of the tank. (It happens!) The cover should accommodate tubing for filters, heating, and air exchange, have an opening through which to feed the fish, and include built-in lights that shine down into the water, nurturing plants and increasing visibility.

Location

Let's start with where *not* to put your fish tank: next to a window or anywhere else where it will get direct sunlight, which can quickly heat the water inside to dangerous levels and promote the growth of unwanted algae.

Place the tank near an electrical outlet if possible. That will save the hassle of unsightly extension cords. Also choose a surface or stand that's level with the ground, otherwise excessive pressure will build on the lower side of the tank, eventually causing a leak. Use a carpenter's level (or that bubble app on your smartphone) to check your tank before filling it. If it's off a little on one side, shim it at the corners until it's level, always using a durable shim that won't slip or collapse under the weight of the tank once it's filled with water.

Any aquarium larger than 10 gallons (approximately 100 pounds when filled) will require a sturdy stand to support its weight safely over time. Consult with a professional to make sure you have a stand appropriate to your tank, and look for models with space below to hide away tubing and equipment.

Water

Nothing is more important to the health of your aquarium than the quality of its water. Ideal tank water is not only clean and clear, it also provides adequate oxygen and carbon dioxide for the fish and plants in the tank.

Fish kept in dirty or poorly aerated tanks will live listless lives, and you'll find that they're much more susceptible to all manner of illness. You'll also have the displeasure of viewing these beautiful creatures through a layer of floating grime.

An otherwise healthy fish gasping for air at the top of the tank is a clear sign that there's not enough oxygen in the water, a problem you must remedy immediately.

Another factor to consider is the relative hardness of the water in your aquarium, which refers to the amount of minerals like calcium and magnesium that it contains. Although found in such small traces that they're measured in parts per million (ppm), these elements can have a big effect on your fish's health. Water is considered very hard if it's above 360 ppm and very soft if it's below 75 ppm, with several grades in between. Using a small, inexpensive digital device, you can determine the hardness of the water you're using, and then figure out how to get from there to the ideal ppm for the fish in your tank. Adding distilled water, with a ppm of near zero, can help bring down the hardness of a tank, as can the use of a relatively inexpensive reverse osmosis machine.

You must also accurately assess the pH level of the water in your tank, as measured on a scale of 1 to 14, with 7 being neutral. Water is considered acidic if below 7, and alkaline if above 7. Most fish prefer fairly neutral water, though some, like those native to East African lakes, prefer highly alkaline water in the 7.5 to 8.5 range. Water below 5.5 or above 9 will harm most breeds sufficiently for them to begin showing serious symptoms.

Frequently changing the water in your tank helps prevent dangerous buildups of minerals, chemicals, and other contaminants, but you have to treat tap water first before it can enter the aquarium because it contains no carbon dioxide and lacks important phosphates and minerals that plants need for proper nourishment. Also, if you're raising delicate fish, all toxins will need to be removed from the water before it reaches their gills.

A brand new, at-home aquarium—including all plants, filters, and equipment—should be run for about two full weeks before adding the first fish to create a stable underwater environment for those animals to enter. That time frame gives plants adequate time to grow roots and aerate the

water while letting helpful bacteria build to optimal levels. It also gives you time to take regular measurements of the acidity, hardness, and temperature of the water so you can watch out for sudden or unexplained fluctuations and eliminate them before adding your fish.

Heater and Thermostat

Depending on the environment you're trying to re-create in your aquarium, you must adjust the temperature of the water accordingly. Tropical fish and plants need water between 72 and 79 degrees, while those from

more temperate climates thrive in water between 50 and 68 degrees. A heater will bring your tank up to your desired temperature, and a thermostat will make sure it stays there.

For most hobby aquariums, an electric immersion heater offers an inexpensive option that works well. Find one with a heating element and thermostat together inside a waterproof glass tube. When installing, make sure it doesn't come in contact with any of part of the aquarium. It should attach to the side wall by suction cup so the tube touches only water. You can also find filters with built-in heaters; they're more expensive and complicated to operate, but they sit outside the tank and therefore don't obscure your view of the fish.

To provide a few degrees of extra warmth for the roots of your plants, consider winding a waterproof heating cable (approved for aquarium use) along the bottom of your tank in a series of S curves. Or stick a heating pad beneath the bottom of the aquarium. Adding heat from below causes the warmer water on the bottom of the tank to rise, creating circulation within the tank that brings nutrients to your plants' roots while washing rocks and coral clean of debris. Too much heat from below, however, can damage your fish, your tank, or both, so use only special heating pads designed for aquariums.

When installing any electrical appliance in or around your aquarium, keep in mind that water and electricity don't mix. To prevent accidental electrocution, all electrical equipment should be connected to a ground-fault circuit interrupt (GFCI) device that turns off the electricity in the

case of a short or a malfunction. Also, buy only waterproof equipment approved for use in an aquarium tank. Consider keeping an additional heater on hand just in case yours malfunctions or stops working entirely. You won't want to wait until morning when the pet store opens to replace it, and neither will your fish!

Lighting

Generally the aim in any aquarium is to re-create the fish's natural environment as closely as possible, but the use of natural light makes for the exception to this rule. Tanks put in direct sunlight will overheat and overgrow with algae. Artificial light allows you to determine the number of hours of "daylight" your fish receive every day. In the tropics, this number rarely changes from about twelve, while fish native to areas further from the equator are used to long summer days and long winter nights. Re-creating these patterns will help the fish in your tank properly adjust their internal biorhythms and thrive as a result.

The plants in your aquarium also require light of sufficient intensity and spectrum to promote photosynthesis and healthy growth. Lack of light can act as a silent killer. Find fluorescent lamps that fit into your aquarium top and run the length of the tank. Plants with high light needs may also benefit from high-intensity metal halide lights, which require a chiller and ventilation to deal with all of the heat they create. Consult a professional before buying or installing them. Better yet, investigate the latest LED lights, which cost less, run cool, and save a lot of energy costs compared to metal halides. LEDs also do a great job of highlighting the coral in your tank and showing off the subtle shimmer in the water.

Filters

In nature, all fish live in moving water. Even the stillest pond has currents that push and pull below the surface. The faster that water moves, the more oxygenated it becomes as it releases carbon dioxide into the air. In the artificial environment of a fish tank, however, if the water doesn't circulate through a filter, it will hardly move at all, meaning this vital exchange of gases doesn't take place.

Think of the filter as the heart of your aquarium, the centerpiece of the circulatory system that brings air, rather than blood, into your tank. The filter constantly moves the water, creating a current in the tank that keeps it from going stagnant. Without it, uneaten food, decomposing plant matter, and fish excrement would quickly build up.

The right filter for your aquarium will depend on the size of the tank, number of fish, and number of plants. Obviously, the bigger the tank, the bigger the filter required to deal with that volume of water. But you must also consider that a tank with a lot of fish in it will require a larger filter than the same tank if less full. For best results, find a filter capable of circulating all of the water in your tank seven to ten time per hour, and don't be afraid of going overboard. When it comes to filters, it's much better to have a little more than you need, rather than a little less, particularly if you plan to add more fish as you go or might move up to a larger aquarium at some point in the future.

To function properly, a filter must be cleaned and replaced regularly. How often depends on the size of the tank, number of fish, what you're feeding them, and how much of it goes uneaten. A clogged filter won't stop working entirely, but its ability to clean the water greatly diminishes. It's up to you to check that it's functioning regularly as part of a set maintenance schedule. If additional aeration is required beyond what the filter provides, special air stones can be installed. Powered by the air pump, they sit below the surface and bubble away.

Gravel

Gravel forms the literal base of your aquarium. Saltwater tanks require a special type of gravel to help maintain their pH levels, so don't assume all small rocks are the same.

Buy enough gravel to lay a 2- to 3-inch layer on the bottom panel of the aquarium. It should be loose and well aerated, so get gravel at least 1 to 2 millimeters in diameter. Sand and other finer ground material should be avoided because it will pack down with no room for air to move through it and reach your plants' roots. Finer materials can also float along in the current and clog filters.

Vigorously wash all gravel—except live substrates—before you add it to the tank. Fill a bucket ¼ of the way with gravel, top it off with water, and then agitate it thoroughly. Then drain the water from the bucket. Repeat this process several times until the water remains clear even after agitation.

Rocks

By giving fish places to hide, swim around, and defend, rocks play an important role in the life of an aquarium. They're also a great place for tiny creatures to take refuge and for beneficial algae to grow. Some rocks can raise a tank's acidity or leach calcium into the water, however, so choose carefully if either of these will pose a problem. Also, like gravel, rocks must be washed before they are used. Discard any that break apart easily during cleaning.

Some fish, like the bottom-dwelling catfish, enjoy a cave built of rocks or wood where they can hide. For more aggressive fish, you can use rocks to create separate "territories," rather than risk them fighting one another for one large common space. Clay pots can also serve as a cheap and effective "territory."

Plants

We tend to call them *fish* tanks, but, like tiny underwater bonsai trees, the plants that you cultivate in your aquarium can hold endless fascination with their delicate beauty and shouldn't be overlooked. Aquatic plants also play a vital role in keeping an aquarium healthy and balanced by absorbing the CO_2 output of fish and turning it back into oxygen.

Unlike plants on dry land, aquarium plants absorb nutrients directly from the water, so you don't feed the roots, as with most plants. You just have to make sure the water in the tank is properly filtered. Remember to choose plants well adapted to living in water of the same temperature and acidity as the fish you're keeping. You also need to consider light intensity since some plants require less light than others.

In return, healthy aquatic plants will absorb unwanted nitrogen and grow roots that aerate the gravel at the bottom of the tank. Plants can also be arranged to provide shelter for small, weak fish, shade a part of the aquarium for varieties that prefer darker waters, and even promote spawning.

Before buying and installing aquatic plants, first make sure everything's ready in the tank for their arrival. Inspect the plants carefully, avoiding any with signs of mold, rot, wilt, snails, or physical deformity. Thoroughly clean the rest, including the roots, which should be light or even white. Remove dark, dry, or flaccid roots with a sharp knife. Then trim off about one third of the healthy roots, being careful not to damage them. This will stimulate new growth, helping the plants to take hold quickly in their new environment at the bottom of your tank.

Most aquatic plants can be propagated by taking a rooted cutting and reestablishing it elsewhere in the tank, a great way to build up the plant life in your aquarium without additional cost. To keep them healthy once established, remove all dead or dying plant matter at least once each week. Carefully clear any debris that may have collected on stems or leaves. Prune any plants that begin to constrict proper flow in the tank or compete with neighboring vegetation.

Properly cared for, aquatic plants seldom present problems. Those that turn frail and have yellow leaves are suffering from light deficiency. Stunted growth often stems from carbon dioxide deficiency. Yellow leaves with green veins indicate manganese deficiency (from improper fertilizing). Brown and black tops usually mean too much iron.

As with maintaining the health of any living thing, the best defense is always prevention. Stop problems before they start by adapting the tank environment to your plants' needs and keeping it there. Replace lights when they grow dim; carefully monitor the temperature, pH balance, and aeration of your water; and change that water regularly to hold down nitrate levels. Your plants will do the rest.

Algae

A properly balanced aquarium grows little algae since algae prefers conditions much different from fish and plants, but if you neglect your tank and let nitrogen build to the point that your plants stop growing, algae will happily take over. One of the biggest potential problems in any aquarium, it's a particular risk in brand-new tanks since the filter hasn't yet had time to acclimate.

Capable of multiplying rapidly under the right conditions, algae, if left unchecked, will suck up all available nutrients, hogging all the food and CO_2 in the tank until it completely takes over. Making a timely, accurate diagnosis of the problem will greatly increase your

A close-up of aquarium algae

tank's chances for a full recovery, so monitor your water regularly for early warning signs, and don't hesitate to act appropriately when needed. Based on the type of algae that develops in your tank, you can usually tell what went wrong and take steps to fix it in time.

- Blue-green algae covers rocks and plants due to overfertilization, the buildup of uneaten food, clogged filters, or poor aeration.

- Red-green algae hangs from plants, wood, and rocks when carbon dioxide levels dip too low.

- Gravel algae covers objects in a thin brown coat due to insufficient light and oxygen.

Fish Food

Fish food that comes as flakes or pellets has been specially made to include a blend of all the nutrients, vitamins, minerals, and roughage required in a healthy diet. Always follow the instructions on the package to the letter when using this type of food, but tailor your feeding regimen to fit the individual fish in your tank. Resist the temptation to overfeed, which leads to obese, lethargic, illness-prone fish, and the leftovers end up decomposing at the bottom of the tank.

Also keep in mind that, while using preprocessed food makes feeding time easy and consistent, most fish actually prefer to capture prey and devour it as they would in nature. Source live food from a reputable dealer, since insects, worms, and other critters brought in from the backyard can introduce diseases and parasites into the aquarium that will long outlive their hosts. What's available at a reliable pet store has been raised under carefully monitored conditions that keep it free of these maladies.

Popular options include flightless fruit flies, brine shrimp, earthworms, crickets, and crustaceans. A knowledgeable person at the store can help you figure out which live food will make the ideal special treat for your fish.

You should determine how much and when to feed your fish, meanwhile, based on the size, number, and variety of them in your tank. Carnivorous

fish gulp down as much as they can and then take their time digesting it in their large stomachs; they can be fed once a day or even slightly less. Herbivores much prefer to ingest small amounts of food steadily throughout the day, like a grazing cow. Either way, feeding time presents an ideal opportunity to examine your fish carefully and look for any problems or symptoms that they might display. Learn each fish's personal traits—how it holds its fins, how vigorously it swims, and where it generally spends time in the tank. Any variation from these norms should cause concern and lead to further observation.

When feeding, spread food evenly across the entire length and width of the tank to prevent a feeding frenzy. If you dump the food all in one place, stronger fish will dominate the smaller ones, leaving them with little to eat. Also, nearly everything you add to the tank should be gone within five minutes or you're overfeeding. Giving fish too much food can damage their livers, and whatever they don't finish will pollute the tank. To prevent this decomposing debris from collecting in your aquarium, use a siphon to collect it every few days before it has a chance to build up.

Care and Maintenance

Much like changing the oil and rotating the tires of an automobile, performing routine care and maintenance on your aquarium will keep it in good working condition, prolong the life of your equipment, and prevent problems before they start. That's the best and easiest way to keep your tank healthy, rather than waiting for issues to arise before taking action. The sooner you respond to a problem, the quicker, easier, and less costly the solution will be.

Start by creating a list of daily, weekly, and monthly tasks you will perform, then turn that schedule into a checklist posted next to your tank. This will help you stay organized and on top of everything, but it's no replacement for carefully observing everything that happens in your aquarium.

Also, no one schedule can serve for every setup. The size and type of tank and the number, size, and variety of fish, plants, and marine life within

it will greatly effect how much effort will need to go into maintaining optimal conditions. You may need a period of trial and error to get things dialed in right, especially with a new tank. Err toward more maintenance rather than less until you get a feel for your particular aquarium and its needs.

For daily maintenance, begin by determining how much and how often to feed the fish. Consulting with a professional will help. Also, do a daily equipment check to make sure all filters, pumps, and lights continue to operate properly. Check the temperature and pH of the water, making sure it's clear of contaminants, debris, and unpleasant odors. Look over every fish and animal in the tank for any signs of ill health, especially at feeding time. A normally active fish that looks listless or hides should raise warning flags.

Weekly maintenance is a little more intense, so pick a time when you're free of distractions. Remember: Having an aquarium is a hobby, not a job, so if you don't enjoy the idea of constantly cleaning and improving your tank, maybe take up birdwatching instead. For the rest of us, this weekly maintenance session will allow you to immerse yourself fully in the underwater world of the aquarium and its inhabitants.

If you share the tank with your children, parents, or roommates, gather everyone together to share the work and the fun. If you keep the tank yourself, ignore your phone and computer in favor of the analog experience of real living animals. Put on music you enjoy, pour a favorite beverage, and start by simply watching your tank for about fifteen minutes. Aside from feeling your stress levels rapidly decline, this will give you a chance to see inside your tank as it normally exists, when your fish no longer feel that they're being observed. Keep a log of how each fish behaves so you can refer back to it if you notice any changes over time. Even subtle alterations in behavior can offer important clues to their overall health and help you treat potential deficiencies or diseases right away.

If any algae has built up on the front pane of the aquarium, clean it carefully. Look through the tank from the side, noting any small floating

algae before it becomes easily noticeable (and hard to handle). Then turn off all the lights in the room, including the aquarium light, and shine a flashlight into the tank. If the water appears as to have dust floating in it, you likely have a buildup of bacteria that needs to be addressed quickly.

Take detailed notes of the water's pH, relative hardness, and nitrite levels, always with an eye for unexplained fluctuations. About once every month, clean or replace your filter, and change out around 30 percent of the water in the tank to keep it fresh, or change out 10 percent of the water weekly for a more stable environment.

To siphon off debris, use a hose and bucket system. Position the bucket in front of the aquarium, and put one end of the hose in the tank. Suck quickly on the bucket-end of the hose but remove your mouth before any of the (terrible tasting!) aquarium water reaches your lips. While letting the water flow into the bucket, use the aquarium end of the tube to suck up any detritus in the tank. Then run the hose along the bottom of the aquarium like a vacuum cleaner, being careful not to suck up any of the gravel or even smaller fish. Finally, clean off the intakes on all of your filters from the outside.

When using this siphoning method of cleaning the tank, you'll generally need to replace up to 30 percent of the water volume to make up for what ends up in the bucket. That's good because it will help keep the water fresh and clean. If you don't get a chance to do this for a month or more, you may need to replace up to three-quarters of the water. Never replace more than that at any one time, otherwise you may shock your plants and animals by exposing them to a wholly unfamiliar environment.

Also, add and remove water from your tanks slowly and gradually to avoid producing air bubbles that can stick to surfaces within the tank, including your fish, potentially causing serious problems. When adding water to the aquarium, pour it into the palm of your hand, with your fingers spread, to diffuse the force of its impact. Otherwise, you can disturb the gravel at the bottom enough to damage your plants.

Begin preparing the new water that will fill your tank the day *before* you plan to add it. Letting tap water sit idle in a container with an open top allows the municipally added chlorine to evaporate out of it. Special

products for treating aquarium water are also available. Use a small aquarium heater and an air stone to raise the temperature of your new water to match what's already in the tank and thoroughly aerate it. Again, this will keep the environment for your fish as stable as possible during the exchange.

Maintaining this homeostasis is also the reason that you never replace the water and change the filters in your aquarium at the same time. Both can greatly reduce the levels of certain beneficial bacteria in the tank, which take some time to build back up. Always wait at least one week between these two maintenance chores—unless a filter stops working entirely, in which case clean it thoroughly before returning it to the tank. Always follow all manufacturer's instructions carefully when cleaning a filter; each one is different and comes with specific directions. To keep from killing off all of the beneficial bacteria that has collected on your filters, wash them in lukewarm water (not hot or cold) and don't add soap, bleach, or other cleaning products. Saltwater aquariums will require washing in saltwater to prevent killing the bacteria.

Finding a Fish Sitter

Sometimes inexperienced aquarium owners mistakenly believe that they can simply dump a bunch of extra food in the tank before a vacation, and their fish will be fine. That doesn't work any better than doing the same with a dog. Food pellets and flakes spoil quickly once they absorb water, so you'll need to make special arrangements for the care of your fish anytime you leave home for more than a day or two.

If you have to leave your aquarium for an extended period, make sure you find someone to take over its care well in advance of your departure so you don't get stuck desperately looking at the last moment. Make sure your temporary caregiver understands all of the time, money, and effort you have put into your tank and more importantly that you care for your fish with the same level of concern as a dog or cat owner. (You can also install automatic feeders to keep feedings consistent and on schedule.)

If possible, invite this person over a few days before your departure so you can demonstrate how your aquarium works and what to do should

something break down. Include a primer on the proper functioning of the pump, filter, lights, and other equipment and instructions on what to do should any of them stop working. This advance visit will also help your caretaker get familiar with all of the fish and marine life in the tank in advance, so it will be easier to notice if any of them starts acting strangely.

Make a list of clear, detailed instructions explaining everything you expect to happen while you're gone. Include your own phone number of course but also the contact info for your vet or a local fish dealer who could help out in an emergency.

Fish Diseases

A wide variety of causes can lead to fish diseases, including parasites, viruses, and harmful bacteria. To prevent these problems before they take hold, follow proper aquarium care guidelines at all times, and always source your fish, plants, and marine life from reputable dealers. Remember: An ounce of prevention is worth a pound of cure.

Also, don't crowd your tank with too many fish, which leads to stress that suppresses their immune systems. It's a lot easier for disease to spread in a crowded tank. Any new fish added to the tank should be quarantined in a bucket or some other container outside the aquarium before entering the tank. Fish should be kept in quarantine for at least one week before being added to the aquarium. Pull the water for your quarantine from the main tank as part of routine maintenance to help ready your new fish for its new home.

Disease is also less likely if you limit yourself to fish that come from the same type of natural waters. Think about it: You can create only one type of environment in your aquarium for all the fish to share, so if you have a fish from cold, clear waters in the same tank with a catfish used to warm mud puddles, one of them will be out of its element, which makes fish vulnerable to all sorts of maladies.

In almost all cases, the key to curing an ailing fish, or at least stopping disease from spreading throughout the entire tank, is identifying

the problem quickly and correctly. Just as people exhibit symptoms that point to an underlying cause, you can begin to diagnose an illness based on behavior, like loss of appetite, resting on the bottom, weight loss, bulging eyes, bloating, and protruding gills. Some of these symptoms can be quite subtle, so this is where it really pays to be a careful, consistent observer of your fish.

Take careful note of any unusual behavior and consult with an expert to determine the likely cause and best remedy. It's also a good idea to have some basic fish medicine on hand so you won't have to run out if there's ever a need. A delay of even a day can allow problems to worsen and even spread to the point of unmanageability. For starters, that means having something to combat ich—pronounced "ick" and also known as white spot disease—a common, potentially lethal infection. When you buy your fish, consult with the dealer regarding the most common problems afflicting those breeds so you'll know what to watch for and can have specific medicine on hand to fix it. Secondary infections happen when the first infection or parasite goes untreated and lowers the immune system, allowing a second illness to develop. You have to identify and treat the primary ailment first.

Fish Fights

Many people list peace and tranquillity among their top reasons for starting an aquarium, and stress relief is typically a great benefit of keeping your own tank, but sometimes fights do break out beneath the surface of the water.

In the wild, many types of fish are highly territorial if not outright aggressive, and even smaller, tamer breeds will fight to defend their space. It's no surprise that the close confines of a typical fish tank can sometimes lead to conflict.

A fish that pushes out its gills and fins, shows its length, and gapes at the mouth has adopted a combative posture and needs to be watched closely. Fish fights can be fatal, though not always. Sometimes a stronger fish merely attacks until a weaker one shows submission by tilting its head sideways and lettings its body dangle straight down. The best way to

avoid fights entirely is to select relatively mellow breeds that get along with one another . . . and don't crowd your tank!

"If you start fish together when they're all young, that also helps," Wayde notes. "But add a new fish somewhere down the line, and you just don't know what's going to happen. A fish tank is a lot like five guys sharing an apartment. All five could get along, and they're best friends. Three could be friends, and the other two could be unhappy. One could become the boss and run the other four. Or they could fight and beat each other up. All fish are different, just like people."

Fish fights should be broken up immediately by removing

Two Siamese fighting fish preparing to duke it out

and quarantining one or more of the participants. Closely monitor any fish involved in a fight for lasting damage.

TEN GREAT BEGINNER FISH

One of the best parts of watching *Tanked* each week is getting to see the stunning varieties of fish that we acquire to stock our latest, greatest custom aquariums. Keep in mind, though: We're experts in our field, making a product either for serious, experienced hobbyists or people who can afford to hire qualified professionals to care for their tanks around the clock. Some of the more exotic species you see on TV can surely captivate your imagination with their beauty, but we recommend keeping the most difficult breeds only if you've got the knowledge, experience, equipment, and budget to meet all of their exacting needs.

If you're just getting into aquariums for the first time, certain beginner fish will help you learn the hobby. Maintain a successful tank with some of these first, and you can always extend your collection to include more challenging species later on.

Black Tetras

During the first few weeks of starting any new aquarium, no matter how carefully you administer it, it will undergo a break-in period during which the ammonia and nitrite levels will steadily increase as bacteria grow and convert them to nitrates. Combine that process with finicky fish, and you've got a recipe for disaster.

Black tetras (*Gymnocorymbus ternetzi*) tend to do just fine under such conditions. Native to the Paraguay and Guapore River basins of southern Brazil and northern Argentina, they grow to approximately 2.5 inches

and prefer warmer water around 78 degrees, though they'll tolerate cooler temperatures as well. Available in several colors and markings and known as the black skirt tetra, high-fin black skirt tetra, and black widow tetra, they eat well, stay active, and don't tend to bother other breeds. They're schooling fish, so plan to get at least four so they can swim together.

Tiger Barbs

Another excellent breed for breaking in a new aquarium, tiger barbs (*Barbus tetrazona*) will definitely keep things lively, especially in a larger tank with plenty of room to move around. Available in a wide variety of colors—green, orange, black, and albino—they can sometimes nip aggressively at other, more passive breeds unless you have at least six in the tank, at which point they will form a tight school and largely stick to themselves. Native to the Malay Peninsula, Sumatra, and Borneo, and now found in many other parts of Asia, these fish like soft, slightly acidic water with plenty of vegetation, and they tend to swim in the middle of the tank.

Danios

For an unheated aquarium, the danios family of fish—including the ever popular zebra danio, pearl danio, and giant danio—make an excellent beginner's choice. Active swimmers with powerful fins, they prefer a longer tank in which they can move around nearly constantly. They're also schooling fish, and you'll need at least eight of them in the tank to keep them all happy. Native to the freshwater rivers and streams of Southeast Asia, danios are omnivores that will adjust to fish flakes or live food like aquatic insects, crustaceans, and brine shrimp. They're surface feeders with a strong appetite, so make sure they don't crowd out other fish at meal time. Because they breed so prolifically, they're also inexpensive to acquire.

Celestial pearl danio

Zebra danio

Goldfish

No fish has a longer or more illustrious career as an aquarium attraction than the goldfish (*Carassius auratus*). In fact, some people overlook the many wonderful attributes of this perennial favorite all too easily. Just ask yourself: Why did people start keeping goldfish so enthusiastically to begin with?

The answer is that they have one of the longest life expectancies of any tank fish, they're tremendously hearty, they tolerate a wide range of environmental conditions, and, thanks to centuries of breeding, they now come in an amazing range of colors, sizes, shapes, and temperaments.

Just remember: While among the easiest fish to care for, goldfish do create a disproportionate amount of waste for their size, so make sure your filtration system can handle the load and change the water in your tank regularly. Also, certain imported breeds—like lionheads, orandas, and bubble eyes—require so much more care and maintenance to the extent that they shouldn't be considered beginner fish at all.

Siamese Fighting Fish

Contrary to what most people first assume, maintaining a small aquarium, especially one the size of a classic goldfish bowl, is actually a lot more difficult than dealing with a larger tank. Any problem, from rising temperatures to bacteria buildup, will quickly overtake a small tank, making it a

less than ideal choice for beginners. Still, they can be an inexpensive way to explore the hobby.

If you do go the bowl route, it's best to choose a Siamese fighting fish (*Betta splendens*) instead of an actual goldfish. Goldfish don't thrive in small, unfiltered spaces. Because of their relatively small waste output and natural tendency to stay in one place and keep to themselves, Siamese fighting fish do quite well in a bowl. But keep only one because, as the name strongly implies, they like to fight among themselves.

Convict Cichlids

If the idea of mating two fish and raising their babies sounds appealing, start with a breeding pair of convict cichlids (*Cichlasoma nigrofasciatum*) in a 10- to 20-gallon tank. Females run a little smaller than males, especially in the fins, with pinkish coloration on their sides, so make sure you're getting one of each if you want them to lay and fertilize eggs.

Once that happens, the proud parents will provide you and your fellow aquarium watchers with endless hours of education and entertainment as they make every effort possible to protect their prospective offspring, moving the eggs from one area of the tank to another to keep them safe. Be careful during feeding, though, lest they see your hand as a threat and take a bite.

Named for the prison-stripe markings on the sides of the most common variety of this fish, convicts also come in gold or blue. Native to Central America, they like rock caves to hide out in and will eat almost any type of food.

Green Catfish

One of the biggest challenges facing inexperienced aquarium keepers is figuring out how much to feed a tank, particularly if the aquarium has more than one species. Each fish not only needs a different amount of food,

but they all feed differently, whether quickly rising to the top of the tank to gobble up flakes and pellets as fast as possible or waiting till food sinks to the bottom. Underfeeding fish will leave them hungry and possibly aggressive, but overfeeding can lead to serious health problems and lethargy.

It's always better to underfeed rather than overfeed, but, no matter how carefully you proceed, some amount of uneaten food will inevitably collect in your tank where it quickly decomposes, presenting a bacteria problem. That's what makes green catfish (*Corydoras aeneus*) such an attractive breed for a beginner tank. As scavenging bottom feeders, they're more than happy to patrol the coral and rocks at the bottom of the tank, sucking up whatever little bits of nutrients have collected after everybody else has had their fill. They're also one of the most docile breeds available. They don't start fights, and they're thickly scaled so they rarely get hurt if another fish decides to start trouble.

Guppy

Another classic aquarium breed, guppies (*Poecilia reticulata*) thrive in hardwater tanks with a temperature between 78 and 82 degrees and plenty of plant life. Native to the Caribbean and Latin America, they're available in a wide range of colors and sizes.

You can establish up to three sets of male and female guppies, best kept in pairs, in a 10-gallon tank. Expect them to multiply rapidly once established; females can give birth to live babies up to once a month! This rapid fertility requires planning ahead to make sure you have room for all of these tiny fish, especially since you'll have to remove them from the main tank immediately after birth to prevent their parents from eating them. It sounds harsh, but this important evolutionary function ensures that only

the strongest, most adapted offspring survive to carry on the lineage.

Specially designed birthing tanks offer an excellent alternative. They fit inside the main tank and section off a special area for pregnant females to keep them safe from attack. Later, the babies can be kept in the birthing tank until they're strong enough to survive in the main portion of the aquarium.

Plecostomus

Also known as the suckermouth, the beautiful and hardworking plecostomus (*Hypostomus plecostomus*) makes a great choice for beginners due to its fondness for eating large amounts of algae, including any that collects on the inside panels of the tank. This not only makes for a healthier environment, it also helps ensure a clear, unclouded view of your aquarium.

Plecostomus are generally quite hardy, but it's best to introduce them to your tank a month or two into their lifecycle—not at the very beginning—so they can skip the tumultuous "breaking-in" period. This is also just the time when algae buildup can become an issue, which will train them to focus on this important food source from the beginning of their time in the tank. Otherwise, they'll get used to eating fish pellets, which don't suit them as well.

Native to Central and South America, the most common variety available in pet stores can grow quite large (up to 15 inches), so you must have an aquarium of at least 15 gallons. If they grow too large for your tank, you may be able to trade them in with a dealer who services larger aquariums. A "bushy-nose" variety stays much smaller, topping out at 6 inches.

Clown Loaches

Available in several distinct varieties and closely related to Southeast Asia's freshwater sharks, loaches (botias) are a family of long-bodied fish that resemble sharks only in the shape of their noses, tails, and pronounced dorsal fins. Its striking coloring—with tiger stripes down both sides and scales so small they're not readily visible—makes the clown variety (*Chromobotia macracanthus*) very popular. It's also an extremely adaptable fish, able to get along with nearly every other tropical variety, and it even acts as a kind of interspecies mediator in a tank housing several different breeds of fish.

Best introduced after the aquarium's "breaking-in" period, in a small group of five or six, they're a hardy choice that offers the added benefit of providing a control against an infestation of snails, one of the most common and vexing aquarium pests. Natural bottom feeders, they like a tank with plenty of vegetation, particularly the kind that creates a shady place where they can hide. Don't be alarmed if they spend much of the day out of sight, burrowed under the substrate at the bottom of the tank, or swim on their sides (or even upside down). These are all normal behaviors.

STOCKING YOUR AQUARIUM: FREQUENTLY ASKED FISH QUESTIONS

To succeed, your fish tank must contain a collection of plants and animals that can live together in health and harmony. Typically, this means focusing on bringing together species that share a similar natural habitat, even if they come from different geographic areas, such as the American Southwest (tetras), Southeast Asia (barbs), and West Africa (cichlids). This strategy works because even very diverse species that require the same type of water (warm or cool, hard or soft, saltwater or fresh, acid or base) potentially can share the same tank.

When stocking your tank, make a budget and stick to it, but don't look for a bargain when buying fish. You'll end up paying more in the long run to nurse and replace unhealthy specimens. Instead, source everything for your aquarium from a reputable dealer. Visit their establishment and speak with them at length before making any purchases. If you have more than one retail aquarium store in your area, check them both out before choosing the one you like best. Remember, this will be a long-term relationship ideally and one of your primary sources for information and advice, so it pays to take your time before committing.

Definitely don't buy fish from a dealer whose stock has small white spots or fluffy white deposits on their bodies, damaged fins, dull skin, or bloat in the middle. Also avoid motionless fish and those that endlessly dart from one section of the tank to another. Walk straight out of any store in which the tanks have a lot of algae or the water appears yellowish, green, or blue. That coloration indicates the heavy presence of medication in the water, which makes every fish within the tank suspect.

Find a place with clean tanks, healthy fish, and a knowledgeable staff, but, as Rob Miller from Exotic Reef Imports suggests, don't trust anybody's advice entirely. Instead, "read up and do your homework," pay careful attention to everything that goes on in your aquarium, and never stop learning or trying to improve.

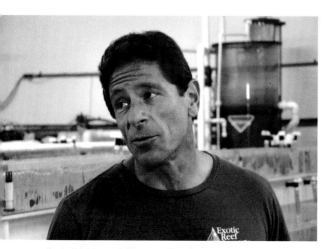
Rob Miller of Exotic Reef Imports

As owner and operator of one of the world's largest marine life wholesalers, Miller imports both wild-sourced and tank-raised exotic breeds from all over the world, including Australia, Bali, Bangkok, Brazil, Christmas Islands, Cook Islands, Costa Rica, Fiji, Guam, Hawaii, Jakarta, Kenya, Malaysia, Maldives, Marshall Islands, Mauritius, Mexico, New Caledonia, Philippines, Puerto Rico, Red Sea, Samoa, Singapore, Solomon Islands, Sri Lanka, Sumatra, Tahiti, Taiwan, Tonga, Vanuatu, and beyond!

A frequent guest on *Tanked,* Miller has helped us stock some of our most impressive tanks with an amazing collection of exotic fish and other marine life. We asked him to offer a few words of wisdom for those looking to fill their own at-home aquariums, and he happily obliged by answering a few of the most frequently asked fish questions from fans of the show.

I'm completely new to keeping an aquarium—how do I get started?

If you're going to invest all of the time and money required to care for marine life, it's vitally important to do your homework before you even walk into the store. Go to the bookstore or a library, find a basic aquarium guide, and read up on everything involved, including basic chemistry, tank setup, animal husbandry, and how different species of marine life interact. Find a good guidebook, and learn everything in it.

When I'm ready to buy fish, how do I find the right marine life retailer?

When you walk into a pet store or aquarium supply store, first look at the health of the fish. If the fish are healthy, the store is buying healthy fish and knows how to take care of them while waiting to make a sale. It's hard enough for beginners to get the hang of this hobby, so you definitely don't want to start with fish that were sick before you ever got your hands on them.

If you see dead fish or even sick fish, walk out. Damaged fins, poor swimming habits, unnatural swimming habits like floating at the top of the tank in a vertical position rather than the typical horizontal position, red sores, white spots, and rapid breathing all signal a sick or improperly cared for fish. Also, a fish that looks emaciated in any way either hasn't been fed adequately or is suffering from some kind of intestinal distress or disease.

If everything looks good on close inspection, track down the store's resident aquarium expert and ask questions, some basic and others more advanced. Ask about things you already know from your research. That way, if the answers you hear from the store's staff run contrary to what you've read, an alarm bell should go off in your head.

What's the first big decision to make when stocking a new aquarium?
Before you start looking at specific breeds, decide if you want a fish-only tank or a reef tank. Do you want to have living coral and invertebrates in your aquarium to simulate a natural reef, or do you want to keep it simple and focus only on raising fish? You have to make that decision first because there are medications that you must use to keep certain fish healthy that will kill coral and invertebrates. You can't keep a breed that relies on that type of medication in a reef tank.

What are some good beginner breeds of fish?

In addition to the beginner fish in the last chapter, if you decide on a fish-only tank, start with some damsels, hearty tangs like yellow tangs, a fox face, maybe a few pygmy angels and a coral beauty. Look for basic, hearty fish.

When you decide to select an individual fish to buy and take home, subject it to the same criteria you used when assessing the store in general, only with even more scrutiny on this one particular fish. Once you've educated yourself, it's not difficult to tell if a fish is sick. Also, make the storekeepers feed the fish in front of you, so you can make sure it's eating properly before committing to your selection.

How do I get fish home safely?

Transporting fish home is easy. The store will seal each fish individually in a water-filled plastic bag. Technically they can survive in there for up to two days, but it's better to plan ahead so you can go directly home from the store, which will minimize the time your fish endures that stressful environment. If you live in Phoenix, Arizona, for example, and it's 120 degrees outside, *don't* leave that plastic bag with a fish inside it sitting on the backseat of your car while you run errands.

When you get home, never introduce new fish directly into your aquarium. Instead, make use of a quarantine system, which involves setting up a small, individual tank in which you can isolate a new fish and carefully monitor its health and progress for a minimum of two weeks before adding it to the main tank. That involves a lot of extra effort and some expense, but it's worth every minute of your time and will actually save you money in the long run.

All you need is a small tank, maybe 5 gallons or so, where you can maintain all of the same water parameters as your main tank, including temperature, pH, salinity, nitrogen levels, and basic water chemistry. This allows you to acclimate your new fish in the safety of isolation without exposing all the other fish to danger should your new acquisition show any signs of disease.

If, after two weeks, you see no visible sign of problems, go ahead and move the quarantined fish into your main aquarium environment.

What the biggest mistakes beginners make?

Overfeeding. Obviously all animals love to eat, and feeding time is an exciting part of keeping a tank, but you've got to resist the temptation to overdo it. Too much food can create serious issues both for your fish and your overall aquarium environment.

Just as with people, overfeeding makes the fish obcsc and unhealthy. Second, if you dump in too much food, the excess will sink to the bottom of the tank and rot among the substrate, releasing toxic chemicals such as hydrogen oxide. The trick is to create and follow through on a strict regimen of numerous, light feedings of appropriate food rather than trying to get by with occasional heavy feedings.

At the other end of the spectrum, underfed fish will show signs of emaciation, particularly those with a high metabolism that burn a lot of energy just by swimming around. This may mean you're not putting in enough food, that they're too disturbed to eat for some reason, or that they're simply getting crowded out at meal time. If your bottom feeding fish aren't getting the proper amount of food because fish at the top of the tank are gobbling it all up, you might need to use a turkey baster to introduce some of the food at a greater depth. Also keep in mind that certain species require or strongly prefer live food. Look into that before making the decision to add them to your aquarium.

Do your homework, then get creative about making sure all of the fish get the food they need delivered in a way that makes sure they get enough. Most fish are skittish when first introduced to a new environment, but the longer you keep them in your tank, the more that shyness will disappear as they grow more attuned to your feeding regimen.

Not changing the water in the tank properly or not changing it frequently enough is the next biggest beginner mistake. Once you understand the nitrogen cycle, you'll understand the way nitrogenous wastes can build up in a tank, which makes changing the water an absolute must. Devise a comprehensive maintenance schedule that suits your tank, and stick to it!

How can I ensure that I'm stocking a tank with fish that can get along?
You need to study. You don't want to keep a predator with fish that will become its prey. For example, if you have a grouper and you add damsels or gobies, that's not going to work . . . unless you want to feed your grouper. Another common beginner mistake is getting a lionfish, which looks interesting, and putting it in with small fish. You'll wind up with no small fish and one very fat and lonely lionfish.

Carefully adhere to two parameters here: Keep mutually aggressive fish away from one another, and keep predator species away from prey species. If you're going to stock a big colorful grouper, keep it only with other predator species, or at the very least, if you're going to stock it with more submissive species, make sure those individual fish are large enough to hold their own and deter the grouper from attacking and eating them.

Here's a simple rule to keep in mind: Anything that can fit into a predator's mouth will be its dinner. If you do end up with an overly aggressive fish, remove the offender immediately and permanently. This is an

expensive hobby, and these living creatures depend on you for their care, so you can't let one fish kill or maim the others without consequence. You're taking a natural environment and attempting to re-create it within an artificial environment that has constraints. One of the biggest constraints is that prey fish have no real place to stay safe. When you're juxtaposing animals in this artificially created environment and something's not working, *you've* got to be the one to make decisions and change the environment based on the greatest good. You can't easily change the tank size, so the easiest thing is usually to change the occupants of your tank.

Should I get tank-raised or wild-sourced fish for my aquarium?

If I had my druthers, I would buy only tank-raised fish. They're generally heartier, they're used to being in captivity, they eat better, and many mutually aggressive species in the wild lose that aggression when raised in tanks because they're used to being kept in the aquarium environment. Certain species that in the wild are extremely territorial, but the same fish when raised in a tank will form schools and all swim together peacefully. The only real advantage of wild-sourced fish is that, at this point, a lot of popular species just can't be tank-raised.

Should I try to add many fish at once to a tank or stagger them individually?

Add multiple fish to a tank at the same time whenever possible rather than staggering their arrival—especially with aggressive species. If you start with a big predator and let it get used to having an aquarium all to itself, it's just going to eat the daylights out of any newcomers you try to add later. If you introduce two fish concurrently, there's far less of a chance of one pummeling the other.

If you do have to add one fish to an established tank, monitor it closely. Any new fish will be shy and skittish, which can trigger the aquarium's natural bully to pick on it, just like the new kid in school!

THE AGE OF AQUARIUMS

A SHORT HISTORY OF THE AQUARIUM

As late as the mid-1800s, most people understood little to nothing about the world's oceans, still widely considered a source of grave danger if not outright evil. Sailors of the era famously delighted in telling tales of giant sea monsters, deadly typhoons, wanton pirates, and frequent shipwrecks that only stoked a primordial fear of the ocean's bottomless depths that afflicted the vast majority of their contemporaries who lived and died without ever spending one day at the beach.

That all began to change, however, in the later half of the nineteenth century, when vast improvements in transportation made the coast an accessible destination for large numbers of previously landlocked people. Railroads in particular led to the popularity of seaside resorts, with a resulting rise in interest in understanding the coastal environment.

Biologists increasingly looked to marine life as a new and exciting field of study. At the same time, the practice of collecting specimens from the natural world became widespread, including seashells and seaweed, which society ladies gathered along the beach, washed in fresh water, and arranged alongside coral to re-create miniature ocean scenes on dry land. A related collecting fad in Britain made ferns desirable enough to have them shipped from the tropics in airtight glass containers, which were later repurposed to bring in live fish for the world's first modern aquariums.

According to *The Ocean at Home: An Illustrated History of the Aquarium,* the basic idea of confining fish to water-filled containers dates back thousands of years. In 500 BC, for example, the town of Agrigento in Sicily built a beautiful fish pond that held this important source of food captive while still connecting it directly to local rivers and streams for a supply of fresh water. These kinds of ponds, filled with saltwater, later became extremely common in any coastal area controlled by the Roman Empire.

The wealthiest of the Romans moved marble tanks—stocked with fish like the sea barbel, a rare and costly variety with poisonous spines—directly into their homes. Around AD 50, the availability of paned glass allowed

An ancient Roman mosaic showing a variety of fish

one wall of these marble tanks to be made transparent, prompting easier observation of the fish inside.

As far back as the tenth century AD, the Chinese kept goldfish in large numbers as pets. By 1369, Chinese emperor Hung Wu's famed porcelain factory began manufacturing tanks specially designed for this purpose, helping to spread the pastime throughout Asia. Today in Japan, countless different breeds and lineages of goldfish flourish thanks to legions of hobbyist breeders who constantly seek to create new varieties with dramatic coloring or unique fins.

By 1691, the first goldfish appeared in Europe, though it took another 150 years before famed showman and circus promoter P. T. Barnum brought them to America. All that time, the popularity of the hobby suffered from one inescapable fact: Nobody anywhere in the world had figured out how to keep fish alive outside of their natural habitats for long periods.

Sometime around 1830, however, French scientist Jeannette Villepreux-Power set up an experiment that involved using a rubber hose to pump seawater directly into a wooden box, creating the first known circulation system to bring fresh air into a fish tank. Richard Owen, director of the British Museum in London, credited her with the invention of the modern aquarium.

Around the same time, a surgeon named Nathaniel Bagshaw Ward developed a system for growing ferns in airtight tanks by allowing a self-stabilizing microclimate to develop within the glass enclosure. In 1841, Ward experimented until he found a mix of fish and plant life that kept an aquarium healthy without requiring a constant stream of new water into the tank.

Jeannette Villepreux-Power

Five years later, British marine zoologist Anne Thynne collected a selection of stone corals from a beach on the south coast of England and transported them to a glass bowl in her London home for easier observation. To keep the seawater fresh, she periodically agitated it vigorously in its container for forty-five minutes in front of an open window, re-infusing it with oxygen. Through this process and the later addition of seaweed to her tanks, Thynne kept her collection alive for nearly three years, a remarkable feat at the time.

Aquariums wouldn't remain restricted to serious scientific study for long. As the price of the necessary equipment dropped and more and more diverse types of marine life became readily available, keeping a fish tank became an increasingly common pursuit among the middle class. Philip Henry Gosse, a pioneering marine biologist, inspired huge numbers of people to adopt the practice of keeping saltwater fish tanks by writing an unlikely bestseller,

The Aquarium: An Unveiling of the Wonders of the Deep Sea, published in 1854.

The book explained in detail how to re-create the ocean inside a glass tank in your very own home. Gosse's aquarium design called for constructing a rectangular glass tank—2 feet long, 1 foot wide, 1 foot deep—with birchwood beading and a bottom panel of slate covered in pebbles, sand, and small pieces of rock to act as insulation and re-create the natural floor of the sea. Then he suggested heading out at high tide on a full moon to scour the coast with a collecting basket, looking for enough plants to supply adequate oxygen in the aquarium, plus animal specimens like mullet, stickleback, goby, periwinkle, anomia, cockles, ascidia, hermit crabs, shrimp, worms, and thick-horned anemone.

Among many important innovations, Gosse's use of flat panes of glass eliminated much of the optical distortion caused by earlier, globe-shaped designs. The birchwood beading also greatly increased the tanks' durability. Over a hundred different species could coexist inside such an aquarium, into which approximately three gallons of fresh saltwater dripped each day from a separate vessel above the main tank.

Even if its readers never started tanks of their own, the full-color, high-quality illustrations of *The Aquarium*—an expensive rarity—showed many people the true splendor of the world beneath the sea for the first time. One reviewer found the whole package so enticing that he recommended keeping it out of children's hands entirely, lest they begin to

Philip Henry Gosse

Anemones from Actinologia Britannica by Philip Henry Gosse

advocate loudly for acquiring an aquarium as soon as possible and not relent until satisfied.

To capitalize on this quickly rising demand, a new emporium opened on Portland Road in London, offering fifteen thousand live marine specimens for sale to the public. They even sold fresh saltwater by the pint or gallon. William Alfred Lloyd, the shop's proprietor, eventually published a 125-page catalog to advertise his wares.

Previously, if you wanted to fill an aquarium, you had to trek to the coast and collect its contents yourself or find someone to do it for you. Now, those same needs could be met easily, locally, and at a fraction of the cost, which led to a huge rush into the burgeoning pastime. Only, like so many fads of the day, it wouldn't last. In Great Britain, approximately 90 percent of the tanks sold during the boom ended up abandoned within a few years as people discovered just how exacting an endeavor it is to set up and maintain a proper aquarium.

Emil Adolf Rossmässler

Meanwhile, in 1856, the popularization of the freshwater aquarium by German naturalist Emil Adolf Rossmässler brought the joys and perils of keeping fish to the vast majority of people who lived too far from the sea for a proper saltwater tank. Freshwater aquariums also proved much easier to maintain, which makes them a popular choice for beginners even today.

In 1858, Henry D. Butler wrote *The Family Aquarium,* a slender volume that promised a comprehensive how-to approach to the hobby completely adapted "to American peculiarities," the first such book published in the United States. Butler promoted the aquarium as a "necessary luxury in every well-appointed household," and an attraction "as chaste as it is beautiful," praising "its neatness and elegance; its fascinating combination of subtle philosophy and commonplace every day facts; its ever-changing, never wearying feature of kaleidoscopic novelty; [and] its tempting peculiarity to thoughtful minds."

By 1883, Hugo Mulertt, an aquarium supply shop owner, fish breeder, and author, estimated in his book *The Goldfish and Its Culture* that approximately two million goldfish were sold in America alone each year, with a value of over $300,000 (more than $7 million today). Around the same time, a group of German immigrants in New York City founded America's first aquarist society, an idea that spread quickly throughout the country.

Initially, with the notable exception of goldfish, all of those tanks featured fish, plants, and other species that could be locally acquired in the wild wherever an aquarist happened to live. In 1869, however, one hundred stunning examples of the macropodus, better known as the paradise fish, were successfully

Adolphus Busch painted by Anders Zorn

shipped to a breeder in Paris by the French consul in Ningbo, China. Within ten years, beer magnate and aquarium lover Adolphus Busch imported the first paradise fish to America after encountering the breed in captivity during a visit to his native Germany and falling in love with the brightly colored tropical freshwater Asian exotics.

Soon rail cars were transporting all manner of imported fish across the country inside soldered cans, 15 to 18 inches in diameter with a 5-inch, perforated opening on top, a method made obsolete only by the advent of plastic shipping bags in the 1950s.

The fish themselves typically were caught in nets in whatever oceans, lakes, rivers, or streams they called home. In some places, a toxic blend of bark and leaves rendered them numb, immobile, and easy to capture. Then they were loaded onto boats whenever and wherever room allowed. Fish make for fragile and therefore risky cargo, and the aquarium supply

business was new and chaotic at the time, so few ships specialized in the trade. When they did take such live cargo onboard, it came in zinc or enamel jugs painted white inside and out to keep the water within as cool as possible while sailing through tropical climates. Each jug hung from a hook, inside a protective box, to keep it from smashing during turbulent storms at sea. To supply the jugs with sufficient fresh air during the journey, the ships' crew operated a special aeration machine by pumping a bellows or operating a bicycle foot pump.

Naturally, all those fish needed homes, so skilled artisans of the day started manufacturing as many fish tanks as the market could bear. Built in every conceivable size and shape, the best custom aquariums of the Victorian era rival the builds on *Tanked* when judged on style and craftsmanship. Some of them even come close to what we now call themed aquariums. In Britain, for example, a lavishly carved "cabinet aquarium" was constructed, with four shelves housing twenty glass containers that grew incrementally smaller toward the top. Another whimsical design combined a bird cage and a fish bowl: The tank was shaped to sit perfectly atop the cage, allowing the canary within to look up from his perch and observe the fresh seafood that presumably he'd never get to eat.

As the hobby grew widespread, aquariums were mass produced with standard designs for tanks that fit into window boxes and terraces, hung from ceilings, and even stuck on the wall like framed pieces of art. Around the turn of the twentieth century, the spread of electrical power to homes made a variety of important improvements possible, including the addition of flowing water into the tank, heating devices to accommodate marine life from warmer climates, and aerators to provide optimal fresh air automatically.

Ironically, as the age of technology and mass production took hold, more and more people moved to cities, largely cut off from the natural landscape, making aquariums ever more popular. For many, a fish tank became a sort of refuge. Today, in our fast-paced, heavily digitized world, the good old aquarium offers a welcome escape for those seeking a different kind of flat surface to behold, one that's not only bright and colorful but also serene and alive.

THE WORLD'S TOP TEN PUBLIC AQUARIUMS

The first public aquariums date back to the middle of the nineteenth century and typically formed part of a larger zoo or botanical garden. It began in 1853 in London with the opening of the Fish House, a collection of more than a dozen glass and steel tanks all housed under one roof. Visitors, promised the *Illustrated London News,* would encounter "a building which the [Zoological] Society have erected for the novel and ingenious purpose of exhibiting, under natural conditions, an amazingly curious and beautiful division of the animal kingdom which, though but little known to the popular observer, people the endless regions of the lake, the river, and the sea."

Within a few years, infamous showman P. T. Barnum installed a small aquarium at the American Museum, which he owned and operated in the heart of New York City. Displayed alongside the skeleton of a "real mermaid"— actually an ape-fish mash-up—the tank joined a legendary collection of curiosities and exhib-

A contemporary drawing of P. T. Barnum's "mermaid."

its that deliberately blurred the line between education and entertainment.

Soon, other, more science-minded public aquariums followed. At the Aquarial Gardens in Boston in 1859, the public encountered forty basins of up to 30 gallons each, arranged in a circle and filled with starfish, snails, sea anemones, crabs, perch, jellyfish, clams, pickerel, sticklebacks, sunfish, carp, bass, sea ravens, flounders, rays, and turtles. In 1866, in Paris's bohemian Montmartre neighborhood, French designers unveiled a stunning aquarium where the public walked *below* the tank, observing the fish and marine life above as if looking up from the depths of the sea.

Today, the world's best public aquariums have grown into massive attractions all their own, but all of them are united in a collective mission to teach visitors as much as possible about the delicate world beneath the water and the many living beings that call it home.

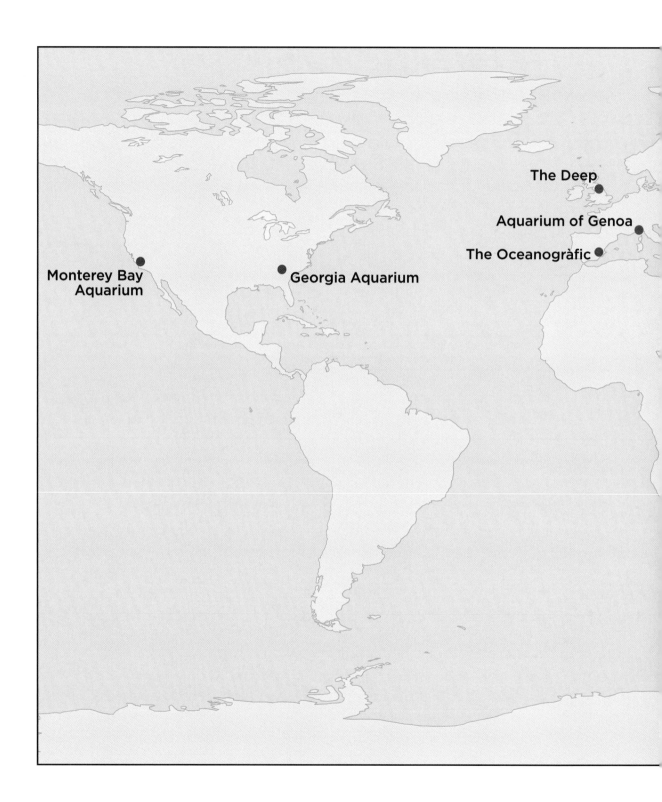

The Deep

Aquarium of Genoa

The Oceanogràfic

Monterey Bay
Aquarium

Georgia Aquarium

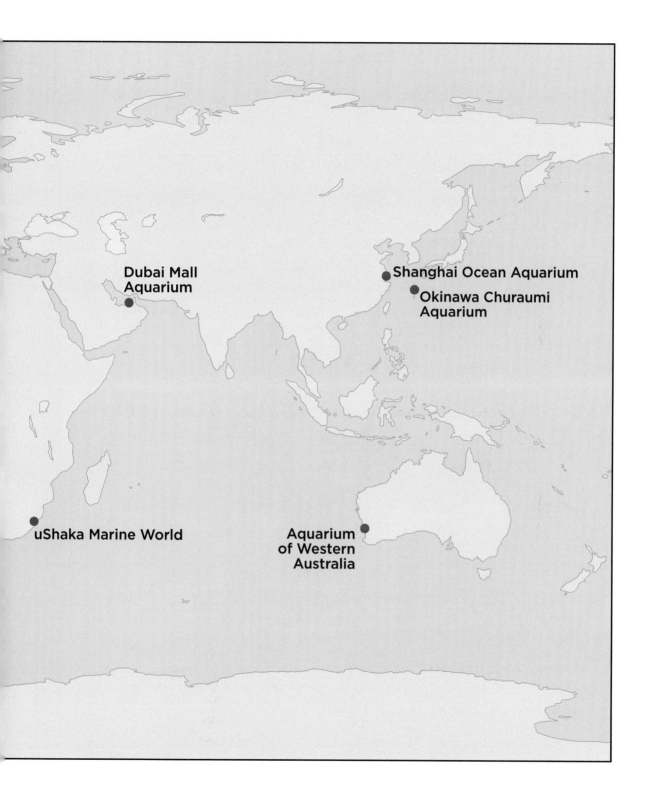

Dubai Mall
Aquarium

Shanghai Ocean Aquarium

Okinawa Churaumi
Aquarium

uShaka Marine World

Aquarium
of Western
Australia

Home to more than 3,500 fish, including Europe's only pair of green sawfish, plus jaw-dropping rays and more than forty kinds of shark, The Deep tells the spellbinding story of the world's oceans via a blend of world-class fish tanks, fun interactive exhibits, and audiovisual presentations. Located at the confluence of the River Hull and the Humber Estuary, the aquarium also serves as an environmental and conservation organization dedicated to increasing understanding of the world's oceans as a way to help preserve them.

What makes The Deep unique, however, is its claim as the world's only "submarium," meaning that you'll view most of their massive tanks by walking through transparent tunnels. Visitors follow this path to encounter distinct exhibits dedicated to re-creating everything from a shallow coral lagoon to the darkest depths of the abyssal plain. There's even a glass elevator that descends more than 30 feet!

TheDeep.co.uk

The Oceanogràfic
Valencia, Spain

Europe's largest aquarium, the Oceanogràfic, situated in the visually stunning City of Arts and Sciences, presents re-creations of the world's main underwater ecosystems to educate and delight its millions of visitors while also hosting important experiments and research to bolster the conservation of marine biodiversity. Separate buildings within the massive aquarium facility focus on the unique environments found in the Mediterranean, wetlands, temperate and tropical seas, deep oceans, the Antarctic, the Arctic, and the Red Sea. The Dolphinarium there runs 35 feet deep and contains more than six million gallons of water.

Visitors will encounter more than forty-five thousand different creatures representing more than five hundred distinct species, including belugas, crustaceans, jellyfish, penguins, rays, sawfish, sea lions, sea urchins, seals, sharks, starfish, turtles, and walruses.

CAC.es/oceanografic

With a chance to explore more than 7,500 miles of Western Australia's coastline in just one day, visitors to the Aquarium of Western Australia encounter the icy waters of the southern ocean, the tropical wonderland of the Far North, and every ecosystem in between, all without ever getting their feet wet. The facility also makes the beauty of Australia's famed coral reefs—long one of the world's top scuba destinations—accessible to everyone.

Featuring more than forty exhibits, AQWA holds more than one million gallons of water, and over four thousand fish call it home. Visitors can explore a special DANGERzone tank filled with a deadly array of marine creatures that sting and bite, or visit the shipwreck coast to watch sharks, stingrays, turtles, and hundreds of stunning fish native to the Indian Ocean.

AQWA.com.au

An AQWA clownfish

Aquarium of Genoa
Genoa, Italy

Located in the old harbor area of one of the largest and most gorgeous cities on the Mediterranean, this 33,000-square-foot facility was built to celebrate the five hundredth anniversary of Genoan sailor Christopher Columbus's famed voyage to the New World. Housed in a building meant to look like a sailing ship, the aquarium's exhibitions showcase the great beauty and diversity of life in the Ligurian Sea, the North Atlantic, and Caribbean reefs "from two perspectives, one the New World/Old World encounter of 1492, the other the ecological awareness of the present day."

Their seventy tanks contain a total of 1.6 million gallons of water, and, with nearly 33,000 feet of exhibit space, seeing it all will take an entire day. If you don't have the time, don't miss the ray fish pool, a particular highlight.

AcquarioDiGenova.it

Shanghai Ocean Aquarium
Shanghai, China

Located in Shanghai's bustling financial district, this $55 million aquarium covers more than 260,000 square feet, divided into nine different thematic zones, featuring 450 different species from five continents and four oceans. Visitors take an underwater journey around the world, starting with an aquarium dedicated to aquatic animals only from China, particularly rare and precious species from the famous Yangtze River.

Then it's on to the mysterious flooded forest of the Amazon in South America, the mangroves and billabongs of Australia, the rivers of Africa, the rain forests of Southeast Asia, the icy waters of the Antarctic, and finally down to the lowest depths of the ocean. Highlights include the Chinese sturgeon, electric eels, giant salamanders, jellyfish, sand tiger sharks, spotted seals, and weedy sea dragons.

Sh-Aquarium.com/en

The crown jewel of a sprawling facility that also includes a water park, a beach, a re-created African village, and other popular attractions, this aquarium ranks among the most visited tourist attractions in one of the continent's most glamorous cities

Now the fifth largest aquarium in the world, it has thirty-two tanks that together hold nearly 62,000 cubic feet of water. There's even a state-of-the-art underground installation built around five shipwrecks, a dolphin stadium with 1,200 seats, a seal stadium, and a wall-sized tank that hosts amazing species like ragged-tooth sharks, spinner sharks, hammerhead sharks, and local cat sharks. Separate tanks house large rays, including local moray species, plus large fish species like giant groupers, potato bass, kingfish, and cobia. Visitors can even take part in an animal encounter, like snorkeling in a lagoon with some 1,500 fish or climbing into a shark cage to visit the floor of the aquarium.

uShakaMarineWorld.co.za

A dolphin show at uShaka Marine World

First opened in 1984 on the site of a former sardine cannery, America's best-known aquarium sits so close to the coast that a series of pipes pumps fresh seawater up into its massive tanks direct from Monterey Bay, over which part of the facility sits on pillars.

Host to nearly two million visitors each year from all over the globe, the aquarium focuses on education, in particular teaching the world about the unique marine life found on the California coast. Monterey Bay Aquarium also created and oversees the Seafood Watch program, which helps consumers and businesses make responsible choices for healthy oceans. Spend the day, and you can watch a live otter feeding, learn about the giant kelp forests, get groovy with some psychedelic jellyfish, and maybe even meet a baby penguin.

MontereyBayAquarium.org

Okinawa Churaumi Aquarium
Okinawa, Japan

Celebrating Japan's natural environment, history, and culture, this hugely popular aquarium has welcomed more than twenty million visitors since opening in 2002. The nation voted on the name, which combines "chura," which means beautiful or graceful in the Okinawan dialect, and "umi" which means ocean.

Visitors encounter a special exhibit displaying over eight hundred different coral colonies, plus a gigantic tank called The Kuroshio Sea that holds the largest fish on Earth, the whale shark, and a kaleidoscopic variety of other species, all viewable through an immense acrylic window 27 feet tall, 70 feet wide, and 2 feet thick. The Okinawa Churaumi Aquarium also houses the world's first successfully bred-in-captivity manta rays, born there in 2007.

Oki-Churaumi.jp/en

The world's largest indoor fish tank—165 x 65 x 36 feet—the Dubai Mall Aquarium also features the world's largest viewing panel (107 feet wide x 27 feet high), providing a centerpiece of suitable size and splendor to a 12 million-square-foot shopping center located in one of the world's most high-end tourist destinations.

With over thirty-three thousand living animals, representing more than eighty-five species, including over four hundred sharks and rays, the facility's 270-degree acrylic walkthrough tunnel brings visitors face-to-face with some of the most fascinating underwater animals on the planet. A special "lunar-cyclic" lighting system adjusts the light inside the aquarium to reflect the movement of the sun and moon throughout the day.

You can gaze at it in wonder during a quick break from shopping or sign up for extras like diving with the sharks, descending to the depths of the tank in a special cage, or an educational program for students and children interested in learning more about marine life.

TheDubaiMall.com/en/Entertain/DubaiAquarium

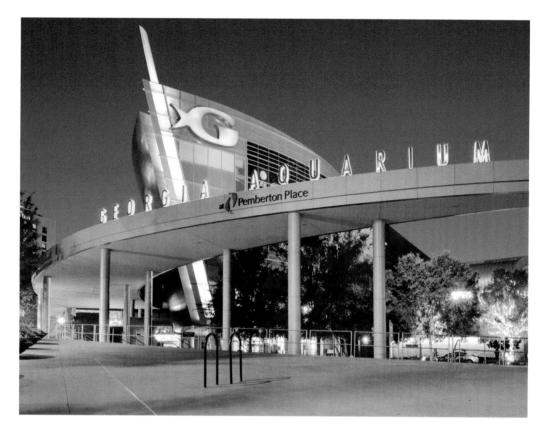

Georgia Aquarium
Atlanta, Georgia

The largest aquarium in the world when it opened in 2005, this facility still features more animals than any of its rivals, all kept healthy and happy in over 10 million gallons of water.

Visitors encounter sixty distinct exhibits that tell a global story about the beauty and fragility of marine life. A quarter of the aquarium's space, called the Learning Loop, provided intensive educational experiences to students, while a state-of-the-art animal health facility, the Correll Center for Aquatic Animal Health, covers another 10,000 square feet, designed by world-class veterinarian professionals and conservation organizations to accommodate a teaching hospital specializing in marine life. The Georgia Aquarium also supports and conducts research on environmental and conservation issues and hosts an educational summer camp for kids.

GeorgiaAquarium.org

FISH FACTS

Test your knowledge of marine life with these fun fish questions compiled by the *Tanked* team of experts.

Questions

1. Growing to more than 50 feet in length and weighing several tons, what is the largest fish on Earth?

2. Native to lakes in the Philippines and seldom longer than a half inch, even as a full-grown adult, what is the world's smallest fish?

3. A small, minnow-sized fish that keeps to seriously deep waters, what is the world's most common fish? (Hint: It's sometimes called a bristlemouth.)

4. Fish have existed on Earth for roughly how long?

5. How fast can saltfish, swordfish, and marlin—the fastest fish in the ocean—swim at top speed?

6. Capable of surviving for over two hundred years, which are the longest living fish alive today?

7. During a single spawning season, a female sunfish can lay how many eggs?

8. You have 9,000 taste buds. How many does a catfish have?

9. If this species gets stranded by the tide, it can hibernate underground for up to two years while waiting for the water level to rise. What is it?

10. Goldie, the world's oldest known goldfish, died in 2005 at what age?

11. How many years does it take the average American lobster to reach 1 pound?

12. Which marine creature has eyes that grow to more than 1 foot in diameter—the largest of any animal on Earth?

13. Which marine creature is the only male of any species to experience pregnancy?

14. One of the most aggressive carnivorous predatory fish species, a group of hunting piranhas is called a what?

15. If threatened, pufferfish take in large amounts of what until they appear several times their normal size?

16. True or false: Fish were the first animals to evolve backbones.

Answer Key

1. Whale shark
2. Tiny goby
3. Cyclothone
4. 450 million years
5. 70 miles per hour
6. Rougheye rockfish
7. 300 million
8. 27,000
9. African lungfish
10. 45 years
11. 7 years
12. Giant squid
13. Seahorse
14. Shoal
15. Water
16. True

AQUARIUM EARTH

Just like the artificial environment within a fish tank, the world's oceans, lakes, rivers, estuaries, and streams need healthy, unpolluted waters to support stable, thriving ecosystems.

Building, stocking, and maintaining an aquarium—no matter its size, shape, or contents—involves creating a small underwater world that must include everything your fish, plants, and other marine life need to thrive in the only home they'll ever know. To do that, you must carefully monitor your tank's vital signs at all times and take immediate action to address any problems as soon as you notice them. Problems inevitably will arise.

Now, let's take a big step back and think of the Earth as a giant aquarium that we all live in and then try to assess the health of its bodies of water. The original source of all life on the planet, these ancient bodies of water collectively represent the most vital natural resource on Earth. No one can live long without clean water to drink, and billions of people depend on the sea and other waterways for their food, livelihood, or both.

According to the US Environmental Protection Agency, more than half of all Americans live within 50 miles of a coastline. Marine-related industries account for one of every six jobs here, employing tens of millions of people and generating $54 billion in goods and services annually. You've probably seen an abundance of seafood at your local grocery store, and you can swim safely at most beaches and inland water sources, but beneath the surface serious problems lurk.

"The very nature of the oceans, their vastness and complexity, hides their sensitivity to abuse by our impacts," the EPA reports on their website. "Often these impacts are delivered to the coastal and estuarine areas by rivers and streams." Keeping in mind our metaphor of the Earth as a giant aquarium, let's take a look at the biggest problems we face and a few simple ways that we can all help fix things.

Pollution

In 2006, the United Nations Environment Program estimated that every square mile of ocean contains forty-six thousand pieces of floating plastic, a number that has grown larger in the handful of years since.

According to UNESCO, "Once discarded, plastics are weathered and eroded into very small fragments known as micro-plastics. These, together with plastic pellets, are already found in most beaches around the world. Plastic debris causes the deaths of more than a million seabirds every year, as well as more than one hundred thousand marine mammals." Swept up in ocean currents, plastic concentrates together. The Great Pacific Garbage Patch, one such concentration, has grown to more than twice the size of Texas and incorporates waste from as far away as Japan and our West Coast.

We often think of ocean pollution stemming from dumping or spills, but it's actually land-based sources, including agricultural runoff of nutrients and pesticides, that account for up to 80 percent of global marine pollution. Rain or flooding often washes away the chemical nutrients used on large-scale factory farms into local waterways that eventually run out to the sea where they help create low oxygen areas known as dead zones. Nearly five hundred dead zones now cover more than 150,000 square miles globally.

Acidity

Just as it's vitally important to consistently check the pH of the water in any aquarium to make sure it remains within the ideal range for the tank, the world's natural sources of water and the wild animals that depend on it also require properly balanced water to stay healthy and happy. Unfortunately, global use of fossil fuels, combined with industrial agriculture and other factors, has led over the last fifty years to a serious increase in the amount of carbon dioxide in the atmosphere, the leading cause of climate change.

The oceans wind up absorbing much of this excess CO_2, thereby playing a vital role in regulating the planet's carbon cycle. The problem arises when all of that excess carbon dioxide reacts with seawater to form carbonic acid, a process that has led to a serious rise in the acidity of oceans

worldwide and similar results in many inland bodies of water. Acidification threatens countless species of fish, particularly if not addressed quickly and effectively, but acidity continues to rise. Seawater that's too acidic impedes the growth of new coral, and, with so many creatures great and small dependent on coral as the backbone of their ecosystems, addressing ocean acidity is hugely important.

Overfishing

"Our seas are not the infinite bounty they appear to be," according to the Seafood Watch Program developed by the Monterey Bay Aquarium in Northern California. "Today, no part of the oceans remains unaffected by human activities, and, among the many factors influencing our ocean ecosystems, few have as great an impact as fishing."

One of the oldest known ways to make a living, humans have been fishing for thousands of years, but about fifty years ago new technology allowed this sea harvest to take place much faster, deeper, and more efficiently than the earliest anglers ever could have imagined. The effect has been a serious depletion in fish stocks all over the world as an increasingly globalized seafood industry catches many species faster than they can reproduce. Today approximately 90 percent of the largest predators like cod, shark, and swordfish have been depleted, and nearly 85 percent of all natural fisheries are overfished or fished to capacity. This situation will have serious consequences for everyone on the planet if something doesn't change soon.

We can all do our part by buying only sustainable seafood. That means—whether saltwater or freshwater, wild-caught or farmed—what we buy must come to market in a way that ensures the health of the environment and an abundant supply of that species going forward. It's a simple concept, really, but navigating these waters involves balancing a lot of complex factors. To make decisions a little easier, Sea Watch developed a four-tiered system for categorizing different consumer choices:

- The Super Green List: A list of wild and farmed seafood that's healthy for people and the oceans.

- Best Choices: Seafood in this category is abundant, well-managed, and caught or farmed in environmentally friendly ways.

- Good Alternatives: These items are an option, but there are concerns with how they're caught or farmed or with the health of their habitat due to other human impacts.

- Avoid: Take a pass on these items for now. They are caught or farmed in ways that harm other marine life or the environment.

Relying on science-based, peer-reviewed, and ecosystem-based criteria, Seafood Watch keeps in constant contact with researchers, fisheries, and other experts to make accurate and frequently updated determinations of total sustainability based on an independent, transparent assessment of fisheries, habitats, management, and other factors affecting a particular species before determining its classification. They've distributed over forty million copies of their popular pocket guides, which they update every six months with any improvement or worsening in the overall sustainability of a species. (The guides are even customized for six different regions within the United States, based on local concerns.) Many restaurants, chefs, fisheries, and seafood purveyors have partnered with Seafood Watch or similar organizations to promote their own best practices and help inform consumers.

For more information or to request your own pocket guide, visit SeafoodWatch.org

How Can I Help?

Serious threats to our oceans and waterways stem from many different sources, but each of us can help combat them. First, you have to learn as much as possible about the natural world you plan to help protect. Then examine your own life and actions to identify ways you can improve. To help you get started on a new, more fish-friendly path, here are a few common-sense suggestions for ways to lessen your impacts at home, work, and on the go.

Conserve Water

From how you wash the dishes (better by hand—only run a dishwasher when it's full) to what time of day you water the lawn (best is early morning, around 3 a.m.), there are many simple and painless ways to cut down on your household's water usage. It's a great way to save money while helping to protect the environment—and particularly important if you live in a drought-prone area.

Reduce, Reuse, Recycle

The best way to make sure your trash doesn't end up in the Great Pacific Garbage Patch is not to make any, but since that's not realistic, focus on creating as little garbage as possible. One great strategy involves finding new uses for old things, like turning an egg carton into a seed planter instead of tossing it out. You can also reuse cloth shopping bags and a metal water bottles instead of using and discarding their plastic equivalents. Recycle properly whenever possible. Right now, Americans throw out twenty-five million plastic beverage bottles every hour.

Also, *always* cut the plastic rings that hold together six packs of soda and beer. If left uncut, they ensnare fish, seals, and other marine life with deadly results.

Use Nontoxic Cleaning Products

For every harsh chemical cleaner under the kitchen sink, a natural, non-toxic alternative like vinegar and baking soda works just as well at a fraction of the cost. The large amounts of phosphorous, ammonia, and nitrogen found in those products pollute local waterways and promote dangerous algae blooms that can kill off plants, fish, and other marine life. Visit Acrylic Aquariums.com to find out more about ATM's nontoxic cleaning products.

Join a Local Cleanup Effort

Joining forces with others who share your concerns will make you feel like part of a powerful movement instead of a lone crusader while providing a great social outlet to meet like-minded new friends. Best of all, at the end of the day you can marvel at a huge pile of collected litter and know it won't end up polluting waterways or harming wildlife.

Research local campaigns to protect the environment near you, and get involved. You'll not only learn a lot by joining with experienced leaders of the movement to save our fragile oceans, lakes, rivers, and streams, you'll also make a lot of interesting new friends.

Contact Your Elected Officials

From your local city parks department to the president of the United States, the people who work in government need to hear directly from you in order to understand and address your concerns, especially when it comes to protecting the environment, where all too often well-funded business interests and their highly paid lobbyists have politicians' ears and the upper hand.

People power can work wonders when applied consistently and effectively. Contact all of your elected officials whenever an issue related to marine ecology comes up so they know that voters like you (their bosses!) are paying careful attention.

The Internet makes it easy to sign up for "action alerts" from various reputable nonprofits working to protect our waterways (see below). They will keep you up to date on the issues and help you send clear, effective messages to policymakers. Social media also helps spread the word, but be sure to use it to make a positive impression on your friends and family.

SAVIORS OF THE SEA

These nonprofit organizations help protect and preserve our priceless waterways and all of the marine life that calls them home.

The Coral Reef Alliance
Founded in 1994 to galvanize the scuba diving community for conservation, the Coral Reef Alliance (CORAL) is a member-supported, nonprofit organization dedicated to protecting the health of coral reefs by providing education, tools, and inspiration to help local communities become passionate environmental stewards while developing managed marine protected areas and sustainable businesses that benefit coral reefs and local citizens. Coral.org

Cousteau Society
To fulfill its mission of "educating people to understand, love, and protect the water systems of the planet," the society founded in 1973 and named for legendary underwater explorer Jacques Cousteau has made countless voyages of discovery in the world's remotest waters, creating books, films, and other educational materials that illustrate and explain the amazing beauty of these delicate ecosystems and how we can all work to protect them. Cousteau.org

EarthEcho International
Founded in 2000, EarthEcho works to inspire individuals to become better stewards of our water planet and enable them to adopt and maintain behaviors more consistent with sustainable living. EarthEcho.org

Oceana
The largest international organization focused solely on ocean conservation, Oceana has offices in North America, South America, and Europe and teams concerned scientists with economists, lawyers, and advocates to work on a carefully selected slate of strategic campaigns designed to help return our oceans to their former levels of abundance. Oceana.org

The Ocean Conservancy

Founded in 1972, the Ocean Conservancy promotes healthy and diverse ocean ecosystems through research, education, and science-based advocacy. Over the last four decades, they've laid the groundwork for an international moratorium on commercial whaling, played an instrumental role in protecting fur seals from over-hunting, pushed for a ban on the international trade in sea turtles, and helped create more than a dozen national marine sanctuaries. OceanConservancy.org

Oceanic Preservation Society

A nonprofit that creates film, photography, and other media to inspire people to save the oceans, Oceanic Preservation Society won dozens of awards around the world in 2009, including the Oscar for Best Documentary for its first film, *The Cove.* OPSociety.org

The Ocean Project

Since forming in the late 1990s, the Ocean Project has grown from a handful of North American aquariums into the world's most extensive network for advancing ocean education and action. More than two thousand partner aquariums, zoos, and museums participate, joining education and conservation organizations in all fifty states and eighty other countries that together serve more than four hundred million visitors each year. The OceanProject.org

Reef Check

Founded in 1996 by a marine ecologist, the Reef Check Foundation is dedicated to conserving tropical coral reefs and California rocky reefs. With volunteer teams in more than ninety countries, they work to create partnerships among community leaders, government agencies, businesses, universities, and other nonprofits while creating a global network of volunteer teams trained to monitor and report on reef health worldwide. ReefCheck.org

Reef Relief

A nonprofit membership organization dedicated to preserving and protecting living coral reef ecosystems, Reef Relief focuses on rigorous science as the key to educating the public and policymakers about the need to conserve, protect, and restore coral reefs. ReefRelief.org

Save Our Seas

In less than ten years, the Save Our Seas Foundation has grown from a small nonprofit into a major player in the fight to save the world's oceans and the wealth of marine life they contain. They fund research, conservation, and education projects focused primarily on charismatic marine megafauna like sharks and whales. They're also the primary subject of *Whale Wars* on Animal Planet. SaveOurSeas.com

Sea Shepherd Conservation Society

Founded in 1977, Sea Shepherd Conservation Society aims to end the destruction of natural habitats and the slaughter of wildlife in the world's oceans in order to conserve and protect ecosystems and species. They employ innovative direct-action tactics to investigate, document, and, when necessary, expose and confront illegal activities on the high seas. SeaShepherd.org

Surfrider Foundation

Dedicated to the protection and enjoyment of the worlds' oceans, waves, and beaches, the Surfrider Foundation was founded by surfers concerned by the profound effect of ocean pollution on coastal areas around the world and prompted by the need to clean and protect them through conservation, activism, research, and education. Surfrider.org

ACKNOWLEDGMENTS

Wayde

I would like to start by thanking all the people trying to save the marine environment. It's so important, and it's part of what makes my job worth doing. I also thank my mom and Shelly for getting me interested in fish and the aquarium business; my wife, Heather, for always standing by my side; my father-in-law for all his hard work and faith—because without him we really wouldn't be here; Brett for his big visions and getting us on TV; Robert for all his hard work; Agnes for all her hard work and for putting up with Brett; Helen for doing such a great job running our front office; Dennis for working on all our big jobs and running our sales team. I also thank the rest of the ATM staff: Without you guys none of this would be possible. We truly are a family business.

On behalf of the ATM family and the *Tanked* team, we also thank everyone involved behind the scenes in the making of this book: Writer David Bienenstock helped us collect our memories, shape our stories, and get them onto the page. Our literary agent, Alex Glass at Trident Media Group, found the right home for the project. James Jayo, our editor at Lyons Press, assembled all the moving pieces, polished them, and made sure everything looked great from start to finish. Cover designer Bret Kerr and interior designer Sheryl Kober expertly captured both our energy and why marine life is so beautiful to behold. Meredith Dias, the project editor, wrangled everything into place and kept everyone on track under seemingly impossible deadlines, and copyeditor Tom Holton went over the manuscript with a fine-tooth comb and asked all the right questions.

Brett

Thanks to my entire family, especially my daughter, Kayla, and son, Bryce, for putting up with the long hours and with me not being able to make it to every event. I also thank all of the wonderful staff at ATM. Without you, none of this would be possible. Thanks also to the production company and all of the

people at Animal Planet. Thanks to Mike and Richie, and a big shout-out to Joel B. Brown.

Heather

I would like to thank my husband, Wayde, for all his hard work and dedication; he truly has made ATM what it is today, and I am so proud of him for setting and achieving his goals. I also thank my daughters, Taylor and Morgan, for dealing with their mom and dad's crazy life and schedule; my dad for everything he has done for me for my entire life—and continues to do—and for believing in Wayde and giving us this amazing opportunity; Brett for dreaming of being on TV and taking the rest of us along for the ride (who would've guessed?); Agnes for being my partner in crime and always making me smile; Robert for all your hard work and years of loyalty. I also thank all the people at ATM who you don't see on TV. Without them, none of this would be possible!

Irwin

I want to thank my son and son-in-law for taking my money, opening ATM, and putting me back to work. It wasn't easy being unemployed for years and sitting at my condo in Puerto Rico on the beach. They gave me the title of CFO and allowed me to do the work of five people, also a plus. I do the purchasing, shipping, contracts, and all the legal work as well as being the receptionist at the front desk, answering the phones, and doing the tours. Some of the perks of the job are going out to two lunches daily and being able to dress as KISS, a merman, or an elf, enabling me to make a complete fool out of myself. I also play referee or mediator to all concerned on the show. As you can see, Wayde and Brett don't see eye-to-eye on most things—but seriously, and putting all of that aside, I am thankful for being able to work with my son, daughter, son-in-law, and the rest of the ATM crew. At sixty-nine years old, I have a lot to be thankful for. Thanks again for making my life what it is today.

Robbie

Thanks to Wayde for making me a part of the ATM team eighteen years ago; Brett for getting us on TV so we could share our art with the world; everyone from our managing team, including Michael Skouras; everyone at Animal Planet, Discovery, and Nancy Glass Production for all their hard work to make it possible for us to share this with the world. Last but not least, my thanks to the staff at ATM, who work hard to make all of our beautiful tanks.

Agnes

I would like to thank Wayde and Brett not only for keeping me always under their wing but also for keeping me employed all these years . . . through the good, the bad, the ugly, and then the good again; Heather for being my wing woman; Irwin for keeping me fed; Robert for his MacGyver-like creativity; and our entire ATM office staff for putting up with our countless antics. To everyone on the *Tanked* production team, you know who you are, what you've done, and what you tirelessly continue to do, and for that I am utterly thankful! And, of course, thanks to our ATM clients and *Tanked* fans. . . . Because of you, our amazing journey continues, and for that this family can't thank you enough!

We'd also like to thank:

At Nancy Glass Productions: Nancy Glass, executive producer; Eric Neuhaus, director of development; and Andrea Gunning, production manager.

At Animal Planet: Marjorie Kaplan, president and general manager; Charlie Foley, executive vice president of original content; Melinda Toporoff, executive producer; and Pat Dempsey, associate producer.

At Discovery Communications: J. P. Stoops, director of licensing; Grant McAllister, licensing manager; Mindy Barsky, design director for licensing; Bridget Stoyko, associate art director; and April George, project coordinator.

PHOTO CREDITS

Photos courtesy of Discovery Communications, LLC, except the following:

Photos on the following pages licensed by Shutterstock.com: i, ii–iii, v, vi–vii, 5, 30 (frame), 79, 98–99, 111, 115, 123, 130, 135, 143, 161, 171, 177, 180, 187, 195, 198–99, 204–5, 207, 210, 213 (top and bottom), 215, 217, 223, 224–30, 233, 236, 238–39 (Phil MacD Photography / Shutterstock), 241, 250 (Phil MacD Photography / Shutterstock), 251 (Jennifer Stone / Shutterstock), 253 (joymsk / Shutterstock), 256, 258 (Cherkas / Shutterstock), 259 (SeanPavonePhoto / Shutterstock), 262, and 267. Fish and aquarium plant spot art throughout licensed by Shutterstock.com.

Photos on pages 13, 18, 20 (top and bottom), 24, 31 (lower right), 58 (top and bottom), 63, 73, 89 (lower left), 96, 102 (top and bottom), 144, and 196–97 courtesy of Wayde King.

Photos on pages 34, 35, 56 (top and bottom), 70, and 72 courtesy of Irwin Raymer.

Photo on page 84 courtesy of Robert Christlieb.

Photos on pages 242–45 and 247 are in the public domain.

Photo on page 252 licensed by iStockphoto.

Photos on the pages 254, 255, and 257 licensed by Dreamstime.

INDEX